Palgrave Studies in Economic History

Series Editor
Kent Deng, London School of Economics, London, UK

Palgrave Studies in Economic History is designed to illuminate and enrich our understanding of economies and economic phenomena of the past. The series covers a vast range of topics including financial history, labour history, development economics, commercialisation, urbanisation, industrialisation, modernisation, globalisation, and changes in world economic orders.

Sonali Garg

The Telegraph and Stock Exchanges

How Innovations in Communications Technology Influenced Regional Exchanges in the United States, 1830–1860

palgrave
macmillan

Sonali Garg
New Delhi, India

ISSN 2662-6497 ISSN 2662-6500 (electronic)
Palgrave Studies in Economic History
ISBN 978-3-031-40406-1 ISBN 978-3-031-40407-8 (eBook)
https://doi.org/10.1007/978-3-031-40407-8

Cover illustration: duncan1890/DigitalVision Vectors/Getty Images

This Palgrave Macmillan imprint is published by the registered company Springer Nature Switzerland AG
The registered company address is: Gewerbestrasse 11, 6330 Cham, Switzerland

Paper in this product is recyclable.

"To my Parents and all my other teachers."

Preface

This book's journey has been filled with gravity-defying drops and unexpected saves. It all began with the research I conducted while writing my PhD thesis. How did I come up with the concept? I decided to pursue industrial organization, finance, and economic history as fields of research. This helped narrow down my research to the history of financial markets in the US.

The New York Stock Exchange (NYSE) was the pre-eminent exchange in the US at the time, and I wished to explore its rise. Discussions at an NBER Summer Institute helped identify 1830 to 1865 as a potential period of interest, as very little data-based analysis had previously been done for this period. The stock exchanges in Boston and Philadelphia were important exchanges and would have been potential competitors, given their physical proximity to New York.

I began to search for price and volume data (to compare the size of exchanges and decide when the NYSE became larger than Boston and Philadelphia) and for bid-ask spread data (to see if the more efficient exchange became the pre-eminent exchange).

The price and volume data were relatively easy to get; the bid-ask spread data proved a different story.

The Hunt's Merchant Magazine was suggested as a source. I ordered a copy through the Inter-Library Loan Facility at my university. (I would like to thank whoever set up this fantastic system. It is like a gourmet smorgasbord for an academician. The idea that, as a student, I could access any book in any library in the US for free, by just walking across to the library and filling out a form, was truly mind-blowing; it still is.) I still remember the day an edition of Hunt's Merchants' Magazine arrived at the library. I walked across the university Oval in the blistering cold to get it. Rushing back to my office, I was excited to find out if the book had bid-ask spread data. Unwilling to wait till I reached my office, I sat down on a snow-covered platform and opened the book. I didn't have gloves on me, and my fingers were already stiff from the cold. Rifling through the pages, I discovered there was no bid-ask spread data.

Someone suggested that the Smithsonian Museum in Washington, DC, might have the data I was seeking. I visited in person. I still remember walking past the display case with Dorothy's shoes from the Wizard of Oz. The Smithsonian did not have it either.

At this point, I had been searching for the data for two years. I considered choosing another topic, but Prof. Steckel (my advisor) assured me that, if I could not find the bid-ask spread data, I could still draw useful insight from the data on price and volume.

At some stage, I got in touch with the New York Stock Exchange. They confirmed they had bid-ask spread data. I went to the exchange with a printed copy of a list they had sent and requested the data for the NYSE for 1830-1860. They had bid-ask spread data, but not for the years that I was seeking. In my excitement in learning that someone had bid-ask spread data, I had not read the list carefully.

I left the NYSE building and called Prof. Steckel from a public payphone. I informed him of what had happened. He asked me how much of time I had left before I needed to get to the airport to fly back to Columbus, Ohio. I said that I had a few hours. Prof Steckel suggested I check out the collection at the New York Public Library (NYPL).

Though it seemed highly unlikely to me that a public library would have the data that researchers had spent decades trying to locate, I made my way to the NYPL. Once there, I located the newspaper archives and asked if they had financial newspapers for years between 1830 and 1865. They waved toward a wall with several journals and said, "Yes, we have several financial and trade journals for each of those years. Which year and which journal would you like?"

I looked at the wall. There were so many choices, and I had just a short amount of time before I needed to take the Subway to get to the airport. I had time to look through just one journal. I looked hard at the journals listed and picked one. I took the microfilm reels to a small room with a microfilm reader.

For those of you who may not be familiar with the process, a microfilm records images on a roll. This is wrapped around a spool. To view the images, you push the roll onto a small rod on a microfilm reader machine. You then pull the microfilm over a piece of glass and insert it onto an empty spool on the other side of the glass. This second spool is also inserted on a small rod. You turn on a light below the glass, and the image on the portion of the microfilm that is directly above the glass gets projected onto a screen above. To view the next bit of the microfilm, you turn a handle that cranks the second spool and pulls the microfilm from the first spool onto the glass; and eventually on to the second spool. When you have viewed the entire roll, you can either wrap it back on the first spool or take the now full second spool and put it back in the box that had the first spool.

I started scrolling through the microfilm rolls, going chronologically. I scrolled through several spools. I was only finding price and volume data. I looked at my watch. If I wanted to use public transport to get to the airport I would have to leave at once.

I was only part way through the roll that I was viewing. I did not have time to finish viewing it. I took off both spools. I decided to roll it onto one spool by hand as I returned the other spools that were already in their boxes. I planned to do this while the librarian was processing the return of the boxed rolls. This would save me a few minutes.

Disappointed to give up my search for bid-ask spread data, I stepped out of the small room where I had been viewing the microfilms and walked toward the issuing counter, to return the rolls of microfilm. A small boy came up to me. He asked: "What kind of films do they have here in the microfilm section?" I said, "They don't have 'films' here; they have prints of old documents and newspapers." The small boy looked confused and disappointed. I said, "Here, let me show you," and I plugged the spool that I had been viewing, onto a microfilm reader.

This microfilm reader was right next to the issuing desk. It was for people with partially impaired vision and it had a large screen, where the images appeared much larger than on the other microfilm readers. I started the machine. The microfilm started rolling from where I had just stopped it a few minutes before. I smiled at the boy, and said "See, this is what they have here. You can watch a bit while I return these boxes." As I turned to return the boxes, I glanced up at the screen. Bid-ask spread data were being displayed. As I stood watching, they appeared again for a later date, and then again, a short while later.

The young boy smiled up at me and said, "Thank you" and I said "No. Thank you. Thank you ever so much." The young boy looked confused. He smiled and walked away.

I turned back to the machine and scrolled through the roll really fast. Bid-ask spread data kept reappearing at regular intervals. I requested some more microfilms of later years' newspapers. I took the unfinished roll off the machine, and with the new rolls went back to a regular microfilm reader. I looked at my watch. I decided that if I took a taxi to the airport, I had some time to look through some more microfilms. I scrolled through several rolls. Many of them had bid-ask spread data. I noted the name of the journal and the years for which the data were available.

I came back to the NYPL several times after that to find more bid-ask spread data for the NYSE. I also visited the Boston Public Library and the Free Library of Philadelphia to find bid-ask spread data for their cities' exchanges.

Analysis of price and volume data helped establish when the NYSE began its rise to pre-eminence; and this in conjunction with bid-ask spread data helped establish why it was the New York Stock Exchange and not the Boston Stock Exchange or the Philadelphia Stock Exchange that became the pre-eminent stock exchange in the US.

This book is of interest to both Economic Historians, and to a wider audience. While my fellow cliometricians will happily devour each chapter including the data appendixes, others may wish to begin by reading the Introduction, Chapters 2, 3 4, 7, and the beginning of Chapter 8.

Readers with an interest in the history; the modern developments in financial markets; and the potential futures developments in financial markets may wish to read the Introduction, Chapters 2, 3 4, 7, the beginning of Chapter 8, and all of Chapter 9.

Readers with an interest in the current day-to-day applications of this historical research to understand why Uber, Ola, Swiggy, Zomato, Blinkit, and Zepto behave the way they do, or how they may behave in the future, will enjoy reading the Introduction, Chapters 2, 3 4, 7, the beginning of Chapter 8, and all of Chapter 10.

Policymakers and competition law enthusiasts will find the Introduction, Chapters 2, 3 4, 7, the beginning of Chapter 8, and all of Chapter 11 interesting.

Thank you for buying or borrowing this book. I hope you enjoy reading it.

Sonali Garg
New Delhi, India

Acknowledgements

This book combines my PhD thesis with several of its current real-world applications. As I look back, I see so many people who have made this journey possible. How do you thank everyone who helped you come this far? One can only try.

To my teachers at Welham Girls' School, Lady Shri Ram College, Jawaharlal Nehru University, and The Ohio State University: Thank you to each of you. Everything I am today is due to your generosity and kindness in sharing your knowledge.

Thank you, Mrs. Puneeta Nagalia (nee Bhushan), my first Economics teacher; Mrs. Shashi Bisht, my Maths teacher; and Mrs. Jamila Singh, my English teacher. The foundations developed under your guidance helped me come this far.

My professors at The Ohio State University—Dr. Lucia Dunn, Dr. Steve Cosslett, Dr. Bennett Baack, Dr. Hajime Miyazaki, Dr. Amy Glass, Dr. J. Huston McCulloch, Dr. James Peck, Dr. Howard Marvel, and Dr. Tim Opler—thank you for your guidance and kindness.

I would like to thank my dissertation committee: Dr. Richard Steckel, Dr. Lucia Dunn, and Dr. Huston McCulloch. I cannot imagine a better group of individuals to have supervised my research.

I received very helpful comments from Dr. Bennett Baack, Dr. Tim Opler, Dr. Richard Sylla, Dr. Larry Neal, Dr. Jeremy Atack, Dr. Paul Evans, Dr. Charles Calomiris, Dr. Lance Davis, Dr. Margaret Levenstein, Dr. Rene Stulz, Dr. Paul Shultz, Dr. James Angel, and Dr. Eugene White.

I received helpful comments from my peers, Shinichi Nishiyama, Kiyoshi Matsubara, Kiyoshi Taniguchi, Glenson France, Robert Dietz, Rosin O'Sullivan, and Sougata Kerr. I received helpful feedback from my friends, Dr. Shomik Raj Mehndiratta, Dr. Ranjit Nayak, and Dr. Sanjay Reddy.

The librarians at the Boston Public Library, the Free Library of Philadelphia, the New York Public Library, The Ohio State University Library, Harvard University's Baker Library, the NYSE archives, and the library archives at the Smithsonian in Washington, DC, were very knowledgeable and helpful. I thank everyone who helped me search for data during the research phase.

I would like to thank the National Science Foundation for their Dissertation Improvement Grant (Grant # SBR-9806872), which helped support my initial dissertation. I thank the Dice Fellowship Committee (Department of Economics, The Ohio State University) for their Fall 1998 grant. I thank the office staff at the Department of Economics at The Ohio State University for all of their help.

I thank my friends: Monica, Pushkin, Mukul, Anusuya, Ashish, Deepa, Mathangi, Priya, Ajay, Patti, Renu, Sharon, Tom, Suru, Garima, Rashmi, and Sapna.

I thank the Bantra, Gupta, Mittal, Sharma, and Shibbu families, as well as Bhabho Ji's family, for their support and encouragement.

Tom Amrhein, Sharon Schroder, and Jeffrey Yankow, my fellow backbenchers: I can say with complete confidence that I would not have made it through my PhD if you had not been there. I could not have asked for more supportive and fun-loving friends. I am eternally grateful.

Bernard Bashaasha, Celia Tong, Mukul Aggarwal, Darcy Hartman, Radha Kessar, Karan Sher Singh, Srividya, Vinod Menon, and Garima Malik: Thank you for your support during my PhD.

Sunil Jha, Ravi Shankar, Nyima Douglas, Akshay Garg, Hussain Asif Poonawalla, Anil Sharma, Indranil Sen Gupta, and Rishi Mammen Thomas: Thank you for always picking up the phone to answer my questions.

Varsha Vidhyadhar Agnihotri, Ashish Agnihotri, Jeevita Soorbah, Satyajit Sharma, Seema Kakran, Anil Karkan, Sonali Prasad, Roli Kachhwaha, Jayant Singh, Vidyut Roy, Anu Roy, Saroj Gujral Ji, Kenu Priya Atrey, Dr. Sanjay Reddy, and Dr. Julia Harrington: Thank you for your support and encouragement. Rohit Prasad and Divya Prasad, thank you for helping me get reading material.

Friends and family generously offered me places to stay while I searched for data in cities across the US. Dr. Aradhana Krishna Jagadish, and Dr. Jagadish H.V., thank you for a place to stay in New York. Priya Aiyer and Ajay Subramanian, thank you for a place to stay in Philadelphia. Dr. Shomik Raj Mehndiratta, Renu Pavate, and Dr. Ashish Garg, thank you for a place to stay in Boston. Sudhakar Kesavan and Alka Kesavan, thank you for a place to stay near Washington D.C.

Dr. Anirudh Krishna, Dr. Garima Malik, and Dr. Rohit Prasad: Thank you for your valuable feedback on different versions of the book.

Monica Narula, Deepa Bhartia (nee Chaudhary), Rupa Basu, and Namrata Kharga: Thank you for your help with editing the book. Your patience and kindness are incredible.

My father, Lajpat Rai Garg; my mother, Rekha Garg; my brother, Vishwas Garg; my sister, Priti Sanwalka; my brother-in-law, Deepankar Sanwalka; my nephew, Kunal Sanwalka; and my niece, Deepti Sanwalka: Thank you for always encouraging me.

Papa and Mummy, I thank you for your eternal optimism and your unwavering belief in me. By ensuring that everyone accepted and celebrated my choice to pursue my PhD in the US, you gave me the freedom to study as much as I desired.

Dr. Robert Wright, thank you for the many discussions on my area of research and for your valuable inputs to this book.

Dr. Tomas Nonnenmacher, thank you for your valuable discussions on this book.

Thank you to the anonymous referees for your valuable inputs.

Thank you: Kathleen Bonte, Troy Bonte, and your entire family, for a home away from home; Ashish Law and Anandi Law, for helping me out on my very first day of my PhD. You were a beacon of support to a person in a new country.

To my "sisters" from Welham Girls' School, each and every one of you: Thank you for always cheering me on. To all my friends from Lady Shri Ram College, Jawaharlal Nehru University, and The Ohio State University: Thank you for your support.

To my students and colleagues at Kamala Nehru College, The New Delhi Institute of Management, the G.D. Goenka World Institute, Woodstock School, Prometheus School, The Ohio State University, Albion College, and Queens College (CUNY): Thank you for being a part of the journey. Your encouragement and support mean the world to me.

To my colleagues at the Competition Commission of India: Thank you for all your support and the wonderful learning opportunities.

A very big thank you to the team at Palgrave Macmillan, Susan Westendorf, Sudip Saha, and Melvin Lourdes. Meera Seth, Noorjahan Begum, and Matthew Savin: Thank you ever so much for all your help. My editor, Bronwyn Geyer, thank you for your kindness and positivity through the entire editorial process.

Thank you: Dr. Satish Jain, for the constant support and practical advice through the years; Dr. Arun Kumar, for your support and encouragement when I was applying for my PhD; and Dr. Ramprasad Sen Gupta, for your kindness through the years.

Dr. John Devereux, thank you for your support each step of the way. This journey would not have been possible without you. You helped me clarify my thoughts, you were encouraging and you helped me remain motivated throughout the process.

Finally, I thank my advisor, Dr. Richard Steckel. Without your support and encouragement, the dissertation—which ultimately enabled the writing that appears in this book—would have been impossible. As I reflect upon the years of struggle, which most PhDs naturally entail, I realize that the dissertation that I wrote would simply not have been possible without your guidance. Though I was running the race, you were running ahead of me, clearing the branches, anticipating the twists and turns. Thank you for agreeing to be my advisor, coordinating my participation with the National Bureau of Economic Research Summer Institute, introducing me to Economic History stalwarts, encouraging me to ask questions, suggesting the New York Public Library as a place to search, encouraging me to apply for the National Science Foundation Grant, helping me arrange a job when funding seemed uncertain, and, of course, for giving me feedback throughout the process of writing my dissertation.

Contents

List of Graphs

List of Tables

CHAPTER 1

Introduction

Abstract This book is based on my doctoral dissertation. For my PhD, I focused on Industrial Organization, Finance, and Economic History and narrowed my area of study to competition between stock markets in the United States between 1830 and 1865. The NYSE was the pre-eminent exchange in the United States by 1910. I wished to explore when and why this happened.

Keywords Bid ask spreads · Boston · Boston Stock Exchange · Philadelphia · Philadelphia Stock Exchange · Pre-eminent exchange · Natural monopoly · New York Stock Exchange · Price and Volume of securities traded · Telegraph

The New York Stock Exchange (NYSE) is the pre-eminent stock exchange in the United States today. For the very first time, this book explains when and why this happened.

This book is based on my PhD dissertation. I chose Industrial Organization, Finance, and Economic History as my fields of study for my PhD. These helped identify the history of stock markets in the United States in the 1800s as my area of focus.

S. Garg, *The Telegraph and Stock Exchanges*, Palgrave Studies in Economic History, https://doi.org/10.1007/978-3-031-40407-8_1

Discussions with participants at an NBER Summer Institute helped identify the period of 1830 to 1860 as one of interest. Very little data-based analysis had been done for this period. In particular, no one had worked on the bid ask spread data for this period.

As the NYSE was the pre-eminent exchange in the United States in 1995, I wanted to know if it rose to pre-eminence between 1830 and 1860. The exchanges in Boston and Philadelphia were also important exchanges at this time. Given their physical proximity to New York, they were competitors to the New York Stock Exchange (NYSE). Data on these three exchanges are examined, to establish when the NYSE rose to pre-eminence.

The answer to the "when" helped establish why the NYSE became the pre-eminent exchange in the United States.

My research fills a gap in US Financial History. Price and volume of securities traded on the NYSE, the Philadelphia Stock Exchange, and the Boston Stock Exchange are used to establish that the NYSE began its rise to pre-eminence in the early 1850s.

Data on bid ask spreads of securities traded on the NYSE, the Philadelphia Stock Exchange, and the Boston Stock Exchange from 1830 to 1860 are presented and evaluated.

The evaluation of bid ask spread data established that the NYSE was more efficient than the Philadelphia Stock Exchange, and the Boston Stock Exchange in the early 1850s. The telegraph became a reliable means of communication by the early 1850s, and its use to trade securities brought the three exchanges into competition. The NYSE; the most efficient of the three exchanges emerged as the winner in this competition, and began its rise to pre-eminence. Subsequent developments in communication technology further strengthened the NYSE's pre-eminence.

An implication of this research is that when the market is left to itself, the most efficient entity emerges as the winner. This helps strengthen the case for non-interventionist policies when stock exchanges are freely competing with each other.

Stock markets have falling average costs over the relevant range of output. So do other services such as taxi ride booking services, and restaurant to home food delivery services. Falling average costs over the relevant range of output lead to natural monopolies. If the size of the market is large enough, these natural monopolies may be contestable monopolies. In so far as monopolies, including natural monopolies, are of concern to Antitrust regulators, my research can help guide Antitrust policies regarding competition in these markets.

CHAPTER 2

The Telegraph, NYSE, Bloomberg, and Uber

Abstract In the early 1840s in the United States, stock exchanges in New York, Philadelphia, and Boston each served their local market. The telegraph brought them into competition with each other. The New York Stock Exchange located in New York City emerged as the winner in this competition and began its rise to become the pre-eminent stock exchange in the United States. A brief literature review is included. The possibility of a wider applicability of the learnings from this competition is introduced.

Keywords Bloomberg · Boston stock exchange · Competition between stock exchanges · New York stock exchange · Pre-eminent exchange · Philadelphia stock exchange · Regional exchanges · Retail investors · Single market · Three previously independent stock markets

The 1800s were a time of fierce competition between stock exchanges in the United States. This book analyzes this competition and applies these learnings to changes brought about by present-day technological developments.

In the 1830s, prior to the telegraph, New York, Philadelphia, and Boston each had a stock exchange. These were the New York Stock

S. Garg, *The Telegraph and Stock Exchanges*, Palgrave Studies in Economic History, https://doi.org/10.1007/978-3-031-40407-8_2

Exchange (NYSE),[1] the Philadelphia Stock Exchange, and the Boston Stock Exchange. As there were no reliable means of communication between these cities in real time, each exchange served its local market.

The telegraph brought these three exchanges into competition with each other. Three previously independent stock markets became, in effect a single market. If a security was listed on more than one exchange, potential buyers and sellers could choose the exchange on which to execute a trade in this security.

The NYSE emerged as the winner of this competition. It became the place to trade securities that evoked intra city and eventually national interest, while the Boston and Philadelphia exchanges remained regional exchanges. This book analyzes when and why this happened.

Several writers have analyzed stock markets' contributions to their country's economic development. Writers have also studied the level of economic integration across securities markets.

(Bodenhorn 2000),[2] (Bodenhorn 2002),[3] (Rousseau and Sylla 2005),[4] (Wright 2005),[5] and (Wright 2009)[6] discuss how a well-developed financial system, including ***inter alia*** well-functioning stock markets; by linking savers with entrepreneurs, positively impacted the economic growth of different regions in the United States.

[1] The city of New York had other exchanges aside from the exchange now known as the New York Stock Exchange (NYSE). When the term the "New York Stock Exchange;" the term "the NYSE;" or the term "the exchange in New York" is used in this book, the exchange being referred to is the exchange now known as the NYSE. This exchange began being called the NYSE in 1863. Before this, it was called the "New York Stock and Exchange Board.".

[2] Bodenhorn, Howard "A History of Banking in Antebellum America: Financial Markets and Economic Development in an Era of Nation-Building (Studies in Macroeconomic History)." Cambridge University Press 2000.

[3] Bodenhorn, Howard "State Banking in Early America: A New Economic History." Oxford University Press, USA 2002.

[4] Rousseau, Peter L. and Sylla, Richard "*Emerging Financial Markets and Early US Growth*" Explorations in Economic History 42 (2005), 1–26.

[5] Wright, Robert E. "The First Wall Street: Chestnut Street, Philadelphia, and the Birth of American Finance" University of Chicago Press, 2005.

[6] Wright, Robert E., "The Wealth of Nations Rediscovered: Integration and Expansion in American Financial Markets, 1780–1850." Cambridge University Press; 1st edition (1 October 2009).

(Wright 2009)[7] also discusses how prices across different markets, national and international moved together. (Sylla et al. 2006)[8] discuss the level of market integration of three US securities. "Here, we examine three American securities that were traded both in US securities markets and in London for long sub-periods during the years 1790–1845. One is the 3s of 1790.....The other two American securities are equities, the shares of the First and Second Banks of the United States (Sylla et al. 2006)."[9] Their evaluation of the data reveals that, allowing for the time it took to transmit information across the Atlantic Ocean, the markets were well integrated by 1815–1845; i.e., the prices moved up and down together. They conclude that this was due to lowered travel times between the continents and more regular transmission of information.

This book analyses when and why the NYSE became the pre-eminent exchange in the United States. This analysis is applied to the competition between (i) stock exchanges today, (ii) taxi rental booking services such as Uber and Ola, (iii) restaurant to home food delivery services such as Zomato and Swiggy, and (iv) doorstep delivery services such as Blinkit and Zepto.

Stock markets are currently experiencing a surge in retail investors and investments, driven in part by (i) a proliferation of cell phone-based trading applications for retail investors and (ii) developments in financial technologies such as Digital Currencies and Digital Wallets which have reduced the time and cost of transferring funds. The ability to capture, store, analyze, and share data is increasing. The impact of these changes on the market share of an alternative trading platform such as Bloomberg is discussed.

Bloomberg is a news dissemination platform. It is also used by potential buyers and sellers of government issued bonds to find potential sellers and buyers. In addition to discussing the competition between conventional stock markets, this book also discusses the potential impact of Bloomberg's growth on the structure of securities markets.

[7] Wright, Robert E., "The Wealth of Nations Rediscovered: Integration and Expansion in American Financial Markets, 1780–1850." Cambridge University Press; 1st edition (1 October 2009).

[8] Sylla, Richard; Wilson, Jack W and Wright, E. Robert "Integration of Trans-Atlantic Capital Markets, 1790–1845" Springer 2006.

[9] Sylla, Richard; Wilson, Jack W and Wright, E. Robert "Integration of Trans-Atlantic Capital Markets, 1790–1845" Springer 2006.

References

Bodenhorn, Howard "A History of Banking in Antebellum America: Financial Markets and Economic Development in an Era of Nation-Building (Studies in Macroeconomic History)." Cambridge University Press 2000.

Bodenhorn, Howard "State Banking in Early America: A New Economic History." Oxford University Press, USA 2002.

Peter, Rousseau L. and Richard, Sylla, "Emerging Financial Markets and Early US Growth," *Explorations in Economic History*, Vol. 42, 2005, pp. 1–26.

Sylla, Richard, Wilson, Jack W. and Wright, Robert E., "Integration of Trans-Atlantic Capital Markets, 1790–1845." Springer 2006.

Wright, Robert E., "The First Wall Street: Chestnut Street, Philadelphia, and the Birth of American Finance." University of Chicago Press 2005.

Wright, Robert E., "The Wealth of Nations Rediscovered: Integration and Expansion in American Financial Markets, 1780–1850." Cambridge University Press. 1st edition, 1 October 2009.

CHAPTER 3

Winner Takes All

Abstract Falling average costs for stock markets are discussed. Four costs are considered and explained (i) Commissions, (ii) Bid Ask Spreads, (iii) The time needed to find a matching trade, and (iv) The potential movement of price against the entity initiating a trade. All four costs decline as a specific security's volume traded at a particular venue increases. When stock exchanges compete, eventually a single stock exchange emerges as the winner, i.e., as the natural monopolist.

Keywords Bid ask spreads · Commissions · Economies of scale · Falling average costs · Foreign exchange · Natural monopolies · Natural duopoly · Positive network externalities · Potential movement of price against the entity initiating a trade · Time needed to find a matching trade

Stock exchanges have economies of scale. As more and more trades are conducted on an exchange, the cost per trade declines.

S. Garg, *The Telegraph and Stock Exchanges*, Palgrave Studies in Economic History, https://doi.org/10.1007/978-3-031-40407-8_3

Falling Average Costs

Four costs are considered (i) Commissions (ii) Bid Ask Spreads (iii) The time needed to find a matching trade and (iv) the potential movement of price against the entity initiating a trade. All four costs decline as a specific security's volume traded at a particular venue increases.

Commissions

Commissions are charged by the market maker or as in the case of the NYSE, the "specialist." A market maker or specialist is the entity who buys when you wish to sell, and sells when you wish to buy. Market makers or specialists are buying and selling the same thing all day. They charge for this service by charging a commission for each trade executed.

The commission is an upfront "fee" that is to be paid for the execution of a buy or a sell order. As the number of trades conducted by a market maker or specialist increases, the fixed costs that the specialist faces are spread over a larger number of trades, reducing the average fixed costs per trade.

Bid Ask Spreads

Another cost incurred by trading on an exchange is a portion of the "bid ask" spread. The bid ask spread is the difference between the "bid" price of the share of a company i.e., the price quoted by a potential buyer, and the "ask" price of the share i.e., the price quoted by a potential seller.

If for example (as shown in Table 3.1 below), the bid price for a share is \$100.25 and the ask price for this share is \$100.75, then the "bid ask" spread of this share is (\$100.75–\$100.25 = \$ 0.50).

Table 3.1 Bid ask spreads

	Bid	*Ask*	*Bid Ask Spread*	*Bid Ask Spread*
	Someone is willing to buy at this price	Someone is willing to sell at this price	Ask Price–Bid Price	
Original Bid and Ask Prices	\$100.25	\$100.75	\$100.75–\$100.25 = \$ 0.50	\$ 0.50

The ask price is typically larger than the bid price

The bid and ask prices are offered by people wishing to buy or sell the share. As the number of potential trades increases, more such prices will be offered up.

The entry of more potential buyers and sellers increases competition between them. This competition leads to: (i) an increase in the bid price; (ii) a decrease in the ask price; or (iii) both an increase in the bid price and a decrease in the ask price.

Table 3.2 shows the original situation depicted in Table 3.1 and adds a situation where there are more potential buyers and sellers.

The market could move from a situation where the bid of \$100.25 and the ask of \$100.75 (spread of \$ 0.50) to a situation where the entry of more potential buyers and sellers causes them to compete with each other.

Potential buyers then increase their bid prices to \$100.375 and potential sellers lower their ask prices to \$100.625.

This lowers the spread to (\$100.625–\$100.375 = \$ 0.25). As the trading volume rises on an exchange, spreads are expected to decrease.

Why is the bid ask spread referred to as a trading cost? Let us consider the example of trade in foreign exchange.

At any point in time, an individual faces two prices during their foreign exchange transactions. A price at which the individual can buy foreign exchange, i.e., the foreign exchange dealer's asking price for the foreign exchange; and the price at which the individual can sell the foreign exchange to the dealer, i.e., the foreign exchange dealer's bid price.

Table 3.2 Bid Ask Spreads with increased number of potential buyers and sellers

	Bid	*Ask*	*Bid Ask Spread*	*Bid Ask Spread*
	Someone is willing to buy at this price	Someone is willing to sell at this price	Ask Price–Bid Price	
Original Bid and Ask Prices	\$100.25	\$100.75	\$100.75–\$100.25 = \$ 0.50	\$ 0.50
New Bid and Ask Prices	\$100.375	\$100.625	\$100.625–\$100.375 = \$ 0.25	\$ 0.25

This is best illustrated through an example. Sunil is an individual who lives in India and is planning a work trip to the United States for attending a conference. He goes to a foreign exchange dealer to buy USDs ($)s for the trip. The price at which the dealer is willing to sell $1 is Rs. 82.75 (ask); and the price at which the dealer is willing to buy $1 is Rs. 82.25 (bid). Sunil buys $1000 at the ask price. The minute he concludes the purchase, he is informed that the conference is now to be held in Indonesia instead of in the United States. Sunil sells the $1000 he purchased back to the foreign exchange dealer at the bid price.

Buying and then re-selling $1000 cost Sunil Rs. 82.75–Rs. 82.25 = Rs. 0.50 per USD. Thus, the bid ask spread is the cost of a round trip transaction of a single security.

Most people will either be buyers or sellers of a currency at a given point in time. Hence, half the bid ask spread is typically considered to be the cost of this component to a person who either buys or sells a share. As a person is likely to either buy a share or sell a share at a particular time, she incurs only one half of this cost.

Another example: if Sunil had purchased the $1000, gone for the original US trip, and returned home, having spent only $750. If he went back to the foreign exchange dealer and sold back the remaining $250 to the dealer, the dealer would buy these at Rs. 82.25 per $ (assuming for the sake of simplicity that the bid and ask prices had not changed). Sunil's cost of buying and then selling back these $250 would be Rs. 82.75–Rs. 82.25 = Rs. 0.50 per USD.

Time to Find a Matching Trade

Another cost of trading on an exchange is the time taken to find a matching trade. This will decline as more and more shares are traded on an exchange. The more potential buyers and sellers, the lower will be the time required to find a matching trade.

Stock exchanges also have positive network externalities. Each new buyer and each new seller adds value to the market. Sellers prefer to list on an exchange that has more buyers, and buyers want to buy on an exchange that has more sellers. As an exchange grows in size, the very fact that it has grown, attracts more buyers and sellers. This leads to a further increase in the number of potential buyers and sellers, which then lowers the time to find a matching trade even more.

Potential Movement of Price Against the Entity Initiating a Trade

The greater the volume of trade on an exchange, the smaller will be the potential price movement against the entity initiating the trade.

Let us take an example. John is an individual who owns 1000 shares of Company A. He wishes to sell these shares. He wants to sell each share for \$55 4/8 or more. The current bid price for the share is \$55 1/8 and the current ask price is \$55 7/8. This means that someone is willing to buy shares for \$55 1/8 per share. This is lower than \$ 55 4/8.

John can choose to wait till the bid price rises to \$55 4/8. Alternatively, if he does not wish to wait, he can sell his shares for \$55 1/8 per share. The difference between what John was hoping to sell for (\$55 4/8) and what he sold for (\$ 55 1/8) is \$3/8 per share: this is the price movement against John.

If there had been many more potential buyers willing to buy at \$55 1/8, one or more of them might have decided to offer a slightly higher price. The bid price could have risen to \$55 2/8, \$55 3/8 or even \$55 4/8. The price movement against John would then have been \$2/8, \$1/8 or zero respectively. The more potential buyers in a market, *ceteris paribus*, the higher the bid price, and therefore the lower the price movement against the entity wishing to sell. A similar, analogous argument applies for someone wishing to buy shares.

Economies of Scale; Natural Monopolies

Ceteris paribus average costs decline as the number of shares traded on the stock exchange increases. As the size or the scale of an exchange increases, costs per trade fall. This is called "economies of scale."

When different exchanges compete, "size" offers an advantage. If an exchange becomes substantially larger than its competitors, and as a result of this larger size, its costs per trade are lower than its competitors; potential buyers and sellers will move to this exchange. This will increase its size further, leading to even lower costs per trade, and more potential buyers and sellers migrating to this exchange.

If competing exchanges are located in different geographical regions, *ceteris paribus* the largest exchange will eventually become the preeminent exchange for all the regions combined; trading securities from its own region and, the securities from other regions that are of interest to investors of more than one region. The other exchanges will trade securities that are of interest to investors from their own region. In some instances, the smaller exchanges may continue to grow in size as the economy of the region they serve grows.

As costs per trade continue to fall as the size of a stock exchange increases, potential buyers and sellers from other stock exchanges will move to the exchange with lower costs, (which in the case of stock markets, is the largest exchange). Everyone wants to trade where everyone else is trading. Eventually, the largest exchange will attract all potential buyers and sellers.

Left to itself, in a market with falling average costs over the relevant range of output, one stock exchange will eventually become the pre-eminent stock market. The other exchanges will find it difficult to compete for trade in the securities listed on the pre-eminent exchange. The stock exchange with the lowest spreads; the shortest time to execution; and the lowest price movement against the entity initiating the trade, will become the pre-eminent exchange. One exchange will naturally become a monopoly i.e., become a "natural monopoly."

This is what happened in the United States in the 1800s for stock exchanges, and this is what should happen in the markets for (i) taxi rental booking services such as Uber (ii) doorstep delivery services such as Blinkit.

In each of these markets, an increase in size leads to a decrease in costs and the market has decreasing average costs over the relevant range of output. Each of these markets has positive network externalities, which leads *inter alia* to economies of scale.

If the market in each case is left to itself, a single provider of services will emerge as the winner. In certain markets that are very large, such as the market for taxi rides in New Delhi, there may be space for more than one taxi aggregator to become a natural monopolist; hence, there may be a situation of a natural duopoly.

Market conditions can change, and a natural monopolist's position can be challenged.

CHAPTER 4

NYSE's Rise to Pre-eminence

Abstract Data on the size of stock exchanges in 1910 and in 2022 and 2023 are presented. The NYSE is the pre-eminent stock exchange in the world today. It was the pre-eminent exchange in the United States in 1910; hence it must have risen to pre-eminence before 1910. The telegraph became a reliable means of communication by 1852; this helped bring the New York Stock Exchange, the Philadelphia Stock Exchange, and the Boston Stock Exchange into competition with each other. The New York Stock Exchange was more efficient than the other two, and it emerged as the winner of this competition. The New York Stock Exchange began its rise to pre-eminence in 1851–1852, and the process accelerated after 1852.

Keywords Boston · Contemporary newspapers · Geographically closest exchange · New York · Philadelphia · Reading railroad · Regional exchanges · Regional markets · Reliable means of communication by 1852 · Telescopes and flags

The New York Stock Exchange (NYSE) has held the fascination of the United States and the world for over a century. Its name is synonymous with free enterprise and the best of capitalism. It invokes memories of fortunes being made and fortunes being lost. Its origins are however

S. Garg, *The Telegraph and Stock Exchanges*, Palgrave Studies in Economic History, https://doi.org/10.1007/978-3-031-40407-8_4

shrouded in mystery. Until the dissertation[1] (Garg, 2000) on which this book is based, little was known about its early history. This book sheds light on its early history, and what turns out to be a very exciting part of its past.

The NYSE is the pre-eminent venue for trading securities in the United States today, having the largest volume of shares traded on any stock exchange in the United States. It is also the pre-eminent venue for share trading in the world.

Tables 4.1 has the value of securities traded on exchanges. The value of securities (shares) traded is calculated by adding up the value of each security (share) traded. The value of a security (share) traded is = Price of the security (share) x Number of units of the security (share) traded.

Table 4.1 Largest stock exchanges worldwide as of June 2022

Value of Securities Traded (in billions USD ($))	
NYSE	3,094.23
NASDAQ US	2,197.23
Shenzhen Stock Exchange	1,883.23
Shanghai Stock Exchange	1,569.24
CBOE Global Markets	1,473.80
Japan Exchange Group	506.86
Hong Kong Exchanges and Clearing	302.86
Euronext	297.78
Korea Exchange	247.71
TMX Group	217.38
CBOE Europe	190.90
Taiwan Stock Exchange	159.60
Deutsche Boerse AG	126.94
National Stock Exchange of India	123.10
B3-Brasil Bolsa Balcao	118.85
ASX Australian Securities Exchange	106.98
London Stock Exchange	103.67

Source https://www.statista.com/statistics/270127/largest-stock-exchanges-worldwide-by-trading-volume/: Downloaded June 15, 2023
By value of electronic order book share trading (in billion $)[2]

[1] Garg, Sonali, "Innovations in Communications Technology and the Structure of Securities Markets: A Case Study of the Telegraph and the Rise of the NYSE to Preeminence. 1830–1860" PhD Dissertation 2000. The Ohio State University.

[2] Not all trading is through electronic book trading. This was the only comparable data that I could obtain on value of trade. Most data on the size of stock exchanges are on the market capitalization of listed companies.

Table 4.2 Largest stock exchange operators worldwide as of March 2023

	Market Cap (in trillions USD ($))
NYSE, United States	25.15
NASDAQ, United States	18.99
Shanghai Stock Exchange, China	7.24
Euronext, Europe	6.72
Japan Exchange Group	5.60
Shenzhen Stock Exchange, China	5.12
Hong Kong Exchanges	4.70
National Stock Exchange of India	3.28
LSE Group, UK	3.16
TMX Group, Canada	2.92
Saudi Stock Exchange (Tadawul)	2.67
Deutsche Boerse	2.18
Nasdaq Nordic and Baltics	1.96
SIX Swiss Exchange	1.94
Korea Exchange	1.80
Tehran Stock Exchange	1.75
ASX Australian Securities Exchange	1.68
Taiwan Stock Exchange	1.63
Johannesburg Stock Exchange	1.17

Source https://www.statista.com/statistics/270126/largest-stock-exchange-operators-by-market-capitalization-of-listed-companies/: Downloaded June 19, 2023
By market capitalization of listed companies (in trillion $)

As per the data in Table 4.1, the value of securities traded on the NYSE was 3,094.23 billion USD. The second largest exchange is the NASDAQ US for which this metric is 2,197.23 billion USD.

Table 4.2 compares the size of stock exchanges based on the market capitalization of companies listed on an exchange.

As per the data in Table 4.2, the aggregate market capitalization of companies listed on the NYSE was 25.15 trillion USD as of March 2023. The second largest exchange is the NASDAQ, United States for which this metric is 18.99 trillion USD.

When and why did the NYSE become the pre-eminent stock exchange in the United States? This book answers these questions.

Was the NYSE always the pre-eminent exchange in the United States? Was there a time when other exchanges in the United States were larger than the NYSE? Was there ever a time when the NYSE competed with other exchanges to be the pre-eminent stock exchange in the United

States? If the NYSE did compete with other exchanges, what caused the competition and what was the nature of this competition? Answers to these questions are crucial to our understanding of the evolution of stock exchanges in the United States.

These questions are also of topical interest, given the competition among stock exchanges today. Just as companies that were previously regional began to become national in nature by the 1840s, companies that are national today are becoming international. Companies from one country are merging with companies from other countries. This is because as communication costs are declining, it is feasible to have larger companies, and those with a wider geographic spread.

The NYSE was the Pre-eminent Stock Exchange in the United States in 1910

Was the NYSE always the pre-eminent exchange in the United States? Until now, no information had been collected on absolute and relative sizes of exchanges in the United States before 1860. The dissertation on which this book is based assembled and examined this information for the first time, using contemporary newspapers as the basic source. The price and volume of securities traded on stock exchanges in Philadelphia, Boston, and New York were compared and analyzed.

Work by R.C. Michie shows that by 1910, the NYSE was the pre-eminent stock exchange in the United States, being several times the size of the next largest exchange (Table 4.3).

We see that in 1910, the NYSE was the largest stock exchange in the United States, being more than five times the size of its nearest rival and trading more than twice as many shares as all the other exchanges combined.

The picture is similar for bond trading. The NYSE was the pre-eminent exchange in 1910, trading more than 19 times the par value of bonds as the next largest exchange, and trading more than 9 times the par value of bonds of all the other exchanges combined. As the NYSE was the pre-eminent stock exchange in the United States in 1910, it must have risen to this position of pre-eminence sometime before 1910.

The period prior to 1910 witnessed technological changes in transport and communications, including the invention and adoption of the telegraph (1844–1852) and the telephone (1878). Canals and railroad networks expanded in the three decades before the United States Civil

Table 4.3 US securities markets, sales in 1910

	Stocks	*Stocks*	*Bonds*	*Bonds*
Market	Number	Proportion (%)	Par Value	Proportion (%)
NYSE	164,150,061	68.5%	$635 million	90.6%
Consolidated Stock Exchange	32,238,773	13.4%	-	-
New York Curb Market	18,671,438	7.8%	$10.8 million	1.5%
Boston Stock Exchange	15,503,336	6.5%	$32.7 million	4.7%
Philadelphia Stock Exchange	8,341,599	3.5%	$14.6 million	2.1%
Chicago Stock Exchange	894,362	0.4%	$7.4 million	1.1%
Total	239,799,569	100.1%	$700.5 million	100%

Source "Table 6.2 U.S. Securities Markets, Sales in 1910. R.C. Michie, The London and New York Exchanges 1850–1914, p. 170"

War. As the cost of travel and communication fell, the geographical boundaries of what constituted a market expanded. Local and regional markets began to give way to national markets. The hinterlands of firms expanded.

Securities markets experienced similar transformations. In the mid-1830's Boston, Philadelphia and New York had exchanges that were regional in nature. Firms listed with the exchange that was nearest to them. Investors in these securities were local too; from areas in close geographic proximity to the exchange. Very few securities from other regions or those that were national in nature were either listed or traded. R.C. Michie: "The London and New York Stock Exchanges 1850–1914".

As innovations and investments in transport and communications occurred, both companies and investors became progressively more national in nature. Quicker, cheaper, and more reliable information on other regions was now available.

Trading in securities enjoys economies of scale. As more shares of a particular security are traded at a venue, the cost per share of executing the trade falls, that is, there are falling average costs in the trading of securities over the relevant range of the market. For the newly emerging national market of the 1800s, we would expect to see a single exchange emerge as the pre-eminent place to trade a particular national security. We observe that near the end of our period of analysis, the NYSE emerges as this exchange.

Why did the exchange located in New York eclipse rival exchanges in Philadelphia and Boston? In order to answer this question, price, volume, and bid ask spread data of securities traded on the three stock exchanges for the period 1835–1860 are analyzed. To establish the reason for the rise, we first establish the timing of when the NYSE rose to its pre-eminent position. Establishing the timing is crucial for understanding the causes.

The NYSE Began Its Rise to Pre-eminence in 1851–1852, and this Process Accelerated After 1852

Using data from contemporary newspapers, the absolute and relative sizes of the exchanges in Boston, Philadelphia, and New York are compared. Prior to 1850, the NYSE was typically larger than the other two exchanges.[3] Though the NYSE was typically larger than the other two pre-1850, these differences were very small as compared to the magnitude of differences that were to emerge post 1851–1852.

Prior to the telegraph becoming a reliable means of communication, even though the NYSE was typically larger[4] than the other two exchanges, and had lower average spreads, it was not the "national exchange." People based in Philadelphia and Boston would not have been able to take full advantage of the lower costs of trading on the NYSE, as there were no reliable means of communicating between the cities in real time.

The telegraph became a reliable means of communication by 1852.

The NYSE began its rise to pre-eminence in 1851–1852, and this process accelerated after 1852.

Economic theory and logic suggest the opening of the Erie Canal; the population of each city; economic activity in and around each city; the introduction of the ticker tape; and the adoption of the telegraph,

[3] On May 31, 1848, the value of securities traded on the Boston Stock Exchange was greater than the value of securities traded on the NYSE, and on the Philadelphia Exchange.

[4] On May 31, 1848, the value of securities traded on the Boston Stock Exchange was greater than the value of securities traded on the NYSE, and on the Philadelphia Exchange.

as probable explanations for the rise of the NYSE to pre-eminence. This book examines each of these.

This book shows that the shift in favor of the NYSE began in 1851–1852 and accelerated after 1852. The year 1852 is significant because the telegraph became a reliable means of communication by 1852. The telegraph was invented in 1844, and by 1846, Philadelphia, Boston, and New York were linked by the telegraph, though it was only by 1852 that the telegraph became a reliable means of communication. This fact is established in "Law, Emerging Technology, and Market Structure: The Development of the Telegraph Industry, 1838–1868," by Tomas Nonnenmacher (Ph.D. Dissertation, 1995). The telegraph allowed for nearly instantaneous transmission of information, which allowed investors a choice among venues at which to execute their orders to buy and sell securities, thereby bringing the three exchanges into competition with each other.

Prior to the advent of the telegraph, developments in transport allowed some companies to expand their scope of operations so that they encompassed two or more of the cities whose exchanges are analyzed. There were already some securities that were listed and traded on more than one exchange. US government bonds that paid an annual interest of 5%, and the shares of Reading Railroad were two such securities. Further developments in transport and the development of the telegraph allowed several more companies to expand their geographical scope of operations.

In the book "Historical Sketch of the Electric Telegraph: Including its Rise and Progress in the United States." By Jones, Alexander, *George P. Putnam, 10 Park Place, New York. 1852,"* the author discusses a communication system put in place prior to the telegraph. This involved the use of telescopes and flags. This system was not very reliable, as is shown by an excerpt from the book, reproduced below. The telegraph, even before it became a reliable means of communication by 1852, was an improvement on this system.

From the book "Historical Sketch of the Electric Telegraph: Including its Rise and Progress in the United States." By Jones, Alexander, *George P. Putnam, 10 Park Place, New York. 1852.* (pp. 133–135)".

[5]"In June 1848, the Whig Convention met in Philadelphia, and it became extremely doubtful who would receive the nomination for the presidency". It seemed to lie between Mr. Clay, Gen. Taylor, Gen. Scott, and Judge McLean. The day of which it was believed a decision would be made, we devised a plan to get the news of the event in advance of all others. There was then no line across the Hudson River, and when the news arrived in Jersey City, it would have to be sent over in a ferry-boat. We therefore provided a set of flags. That mounted with a single piece of white cloth, was to indicate Gen. Taylor was nominated. Another, with a red flag, was to denote that that Mr. Clay had received the nomination. Two white flags on the same staff was to indicate Gen. Scott as the nominee, and two red flags on a staff were to denote the result in favor of Judge McLean. We took a young man from the Courier Office, gave him a white signal flag, to answer us when we would take our position on the west side of the River. We placed him on a pier near the Cortlandt Street Ferry and gave him the necessary instructions. At about 10 to 11 A.M., we crossed over. It seems that there was, unknown to us, a party employed by a company of brokers, to telegraph the prices of stocks from the top of the Merchants' Exchange[6] to Jersey City. One man would stand on top of this building, and, on waving his flag, would be answered by another man, who would wave a white flag as a token of his readiness to receive communications. The figure of prices of stocks would be indicated by the motions given to the flag from right to left, horizontally, & c., by the operator. The man who received the numbers in Jersey City, would resend or telegraph them to Philadelphia. After I had placed my man at 11 ½ A.M., the brokers' man in Jersey City stepped out on the pier, and waved his

[5] Hyphens used when a word ran over from one line to the next, (due to shortage of space on the original line), have been removed. The word "nomination" is written as "nomi-nation" in the original text.

[6] The exchange now known as the NYSE was operating from this building. Source: "*United States Department of the Interior. National Park Services. National Register of Historical Places Inventory—Nomination Form. New York Stock Exchange.*" "Since its inception in 1792, the New York Stock Exchange has occupied a number of locations. It made its headquarters in the Tontine Coffee House until 1817; in rented space at 40 Wall Street from 1817 to 1819; in three temporary locations from 1819 to 1827; in the Merchants' Exchange from 1827 until it was destroyed by fire in 1835; in three more temporary locations from 1835 to 1842; in the Second Merchants' Exchange from 1842 to 1854; in the Corn Exchange Bank building from 1854 to 1856; and in the Lord's Court building at William and Beaver Streets and Exchange Place from 1856 to 1865."

flag to the man on the Exchange as usual, as a token that he was on hand. Our young man, seeing this white flag waving on the pier, supposed it to be ours, and immediately ran to the newspaper offices, and informed them that Gen. Taylor was nominated. It produced great excitement and was telegraphed east. On reaching Portland, Maine, 100 guns were fired. The eastern line soon after gave out, and the news could not be contradicted. It turned out than Gen. Taylor was not nominated till the succeeding day.

We could relate many other curious incidents in connection with early telegraph operations, many of which are quite amusing.

We afterwards ascertained that a combination of brokers, in Wall-street and Philadelphia, had previous to the erection of the electric telegraph line between New-York and the latter city, established a private semaphoric or *visual telegraph.*

Their plan was to station men on eminences at every six or eight miles, with telescopes in their hands. They were also provided with flags. At 11 o'clock in the Board of Brokers, at the Merchants' Exchange, the prices at which the stocks chiefly dealt in, sold at, would be given to the flag-man on top of the Exchange, who would communicate the quotations to another flag-man in Jersey City, or on top of Bergen Hill, and he to the next, until Philadelphia was reached. The sales in Philadelphia would reach New-York by a similar method. The order in which they were sent, indicated what stocks were referred to.

The flag was attached to the end of a short stick, held in either hand. All the figures could be represented by the position in which the flag was held or moved. Thus, if the flag was held at right-angles to the body, it might be taken to mean any one of the ten digits. When held up directly over the head, it might indicate a second figure. Other figures could be represented by changing the flag to the left-hand, and varying the motions accordingly. When held perpendicularly over the head, it might mean that the market generally was up; and when held down at a sharp angle to the body, it might indicate the reverse. Half revolutions to the right, would give half numbers; the same to the left quarters-and over the head *eighths.*

It was said that news by this plan could be trans-mitted in about thirty minutes. The chief originator and superintendent of the scheme, was said to be broker in Philadelphia, who retired with a fortune." Source: "Historical Sketch of the Electric Telegraph: Including its Rise and Progress in the United States." By Jones, Alexander, *George P. Putnam, 10 Park Place, New York. 1852.* (pp. 133–135)

Prior to the telegraph becoming a reliable means of communication, even though securities invoked interest in investors over a geographically dispersed area, investors usually bought and sold on the geographically closest exchange. National securities existed. An investor interested in buying or selling a security could, in theory, choose among several exchanges. Real-time transmission of information on the state of the markets, and the transmission of buy and sell orders between geographically distant places was slow and unreliable. In practice, the investor did not have a choice among the different exchanges. What existed, then, were several regional markets, shielded from competition by lack of reliable and affordable real-time communication.

The telegraph drastically reduced communication costs. Once reliable communications technology was available, there was competition among the exchanges.

New York benefited more than Boston or Philadelphia from this competition. At the time the telegraph was introduced, the NYSE was the most efficient exchange, having the lowest average bid ask spreads and the lowest absolute spreads on at least one cross-listed security. In addition, it was larger than the other two in terms of volume and value of shares traded. The larger volume and value of trade were an advantage for the NYSE as investors could find a matching buy or sell order faster on the NYSE than on any other exchange. Given the relative sizes of the exchanges, the price movement against an investor initiating a trade would be smallest on the NYSE. Given a choice among several exchanges, investors in cross-listed securities, subject to the costs of transmitting information through the telegraph, would choose the NYSE over the other two exchanges.

As further developments in transport and communication took place, and more securities were cross-listed, the movement in favor of New York continued. Trading data on at least one cross-listed security; the Reading Railroad show a shift in favor of the NYSE.

National securities (such as US Government 5% bonds) existed prior to the advent of the telegraph, but a national investor choosing among several exchanges had to wait until the advent of the telegraph. The telegraph brought these regional exchanges, previously shielded from competition, into competition with each other. The most efficient among them became the national exchange and the others remained regional exchanges.

This book is laid out as follows. Chapter 5 examines the usual suspects. It looks at explanations offered for the rise of the NYSE to pre-eminence. Chapter 6 discusses the data collected and analyzed. Chapter 7 presents the data collected as graphs. Chapter 8 evaluates the different explanations discussed in Chapter 5. Chapter 9 includes the conclusion and a discussion of the implications of the findings of this book on the future structure of securities markets. Chapter 10 discusses competition between newly emerging natural monopolies. Chapter 11 discusses policy implications for competition between natural monopolies.

Reference

Garg, Sonali, "Innovations in Communications Technology and the Structure of Securities Markets: A Case Study of the Telegraph and the Rise of the NYSE to Preeminence. 1830–1860." *PhD Dissertation,* 2000. The Ohio State University.

CHAPTER 5

The Usual Suspects

Abstract Plausible explanations for the rise of the New York Stock Exchange to pre-eminence are presented. These are (i) Population (ii) Wealth (iii) Opening of the Erie Canal (iv) Stock Ticker and the (v) Telegraph. Existing literature on these plausible explanations, and on when the NYSE rose to pre-eminence is presented.

Keywords Boston · Developments in transport and communication · Erie Canal · New York · Philadelphia · Population · Stock ticker · Telegraph · Telephone · Wealth

In order to identify why the NYSE became the pre-eminent exchange in the United States, the dissertation on which this book is based first establishes exactly when the NYSE began its rise to pre-eminence. Prior to the dissertation on which this book is based, there was literature on when the NYSE began its rise to pre-eminence, but this literature discussed the timing of the rise in broad terms.

> In "The Formation of Financial Centers: A Study in Comparative Economic History," Charles P. Kindleberger writes "The rise of New York as the financial center of the United States, winning out initially over Boston, Philadelphia, and Baltimore in the first quarter of the nineteenth

S. Garg, *The Telegraph and Stock Exchanges*, Palgrave Studies in Economic History, https://doi.org/10.1007/978-3-031-40407-8_5

> century, and beating back, so to speak, later challenges from Chicago and St. Louis, is sufficiently familiar that it need not occupy us for long."[1]

The fact that the NYSE was pre-eminent by the 1900s was well documented. Hence it must have risen to pre-eminence before that. No data-based analysis could be located that identified exactly when this occurred. The dissertation on which this book is based analyzed data on the size of exchanges in the United States for the period 1830 to 1860, in order to identify if the NYSE rose to pre-eminence in this time period. Identifying when the NYSE began its rise to pre-eminence helped explain why the NYSE, and not any other exchange became the pre-eminent exchange in the United States. Several plausible explanations, each based on economic theory and logic have been suggested. We first list and discuss these. These are then evaluated based on data.

Plausible Hypotheses: These are the possible explanations for the rise of the NYSE to pre-eminence.

Population: As New York had the largest population in the period under consideration, it would be the natural place for the pre-eminent exchange to emerge.

Wealth: As New York was wealthier than the other two cities during the period under consideration, it would be the natural place for the pre-eminent exchange to emerge.

Erie Canal: The opening of the Erie Canal is offered as an explanation for the rise. The Erie Canal opened in 1825. This led to increased economic activity in New York, so that New York had more economic activity than the other two cities. This increased economic activity required financing, and this boosted the NYSE. This is still the most widely held view for the rise of the NYSE to pre-eminence. Tourist guides in Philadelphia, when taking tourists past the building that formerly housed the Philadelphia Stock Exchange, give the opening of the Erie Canal as the reason for the NYSE's subsequent faster growth as compared to that of the Philadelphia Stock Exchange.

Stock Ticker: The introduction of the Stock Ticker in 1867 has been put forth as the reason for the NYSE's rise to pre-eminence. Proponents of this view say that by reducing the cost of disseminating stock market

[1] Charles P. Kindleberger: "The Formation of Financial Centers: A Study in Comparative Economic History."

information, the ticker tape made information relating to the NYSE more widely available, and this caused trading to move to the NYSE.

Telegraph: By linking distant markets, and allowing people the option of trading on several different exchanges regardless of where they lived, the telegraph led to the creation of a centralized market for national securities, and led to the rise of the NYSE to pre-eminence.

These hypotheses are elaborated upon below.

This book tests whether the size of the NYSE can simply be explained by the level of economic activity in the region. Invariably, centers of economic activity were also areas of population concentration. Therefore, it is necessary to test whether NYSE's size can be attributed to the region's population size.

The Erie Canal substantially increased the economic importance of New York City. It is likely then, that it may have led to the rise of the NYSE to pre-eminence. We investigated if this was so.

The telegraph and the ticker tape were introduced before 1900. Both inventions made it cheaper and quicker to transmit stock market information. As both affected stock markets, it is necessary to analyze their impact.

Two papers analyze the impact of communications technology on stock markets. These are papers by Garbade and Silber (1978) and DuBoff (1983).

Garbade and Silber (1978) discuss the impact that changes in communications technology had on security exchanges. They study the period 1840–1975 and analyze the impact of the domestic telegraph, the trans-Atlantic cable, and the consolidated tape. They hypothesize that these innovations led to greater market integration, an idea they test by examining whether inter-market price differentials for cross-listed securities narrowed significantly after the introduction of each of these innovations. They conclude that the introduction of the domestic telegraph and the transatlantic cable both led to a significant and rapid narrowing of inter-market price differentials, and that the introduction of the consolidated tape contributed little to the reduction in price differentials.

DuBoff (1983) discusses the impact of the telegraph on economic development and market structures. According to DuBoff, the telegraph improved the functioning of markets and led to increased competition. Simultaneously, it facilitated the formation of large-scale business entities. The changes that took place in the industrial structure of the United States from 1870 to 1900 were a result of changes taking place between

1840 and 1860, such as the growth of markets, the expansion of railroads, and breakthrough in communications. The telegraph was crucial for the above three changes.

In his book "The London and New York Stock Exchanges 1850–1914" R.C. Michie discusses the impact that changes in communications technology had on securities markets. He discusses the telegraph, the telephone, and the ticker tape individually, and together, as responsible for transforming securities markets in the United States. He provides the intuition that these changes in communications created an integrated market for securities. He takes the pre-eminent position of New York, and especially its position as the hub of all this activity, as a given, and does not discuss why it was New York and not the other markets. He does mention that prior to the telegraph the NYSE was large without being important.

> "For much of the first half of the nineteenth century the US stock exchanges that existed were little more than local markets, whose level and nature of business reflected the size, wealth and interest of the local population. The New York Stock Exchange, for instance, was largely engaged in providing markets for the issues of New York-based companies or public bodies. In 1820, of the 30 different securities trading there, 28 were local, belonging to 16 insurance companies, 9 banks, and 3 authorities. Only two were non-local, namely federal government bonds and the stock of the Bank of United States. By 1835 the list of securities had quadrupled, largely through an expansion in the number of banks and insurance companies and the addition of local railroads and utilities. The non-local proportion had grown, especially among the banks and railroads, but still remained a minority, contributing only 35 out of the 124 securities quoted. The consequence was that the stock exchanges in the main eastern cities of New York, Philadelphia, Boston and Baltimore remained on par, with New York having only a slight if noticeable lead."[2]

According to R.C. Michie, the exchanges did not trade in isolation, as there were some cross-listed securities. Arbitrage did occur but required substantial price differentials to make it worth the cost and risk involved. Thus, large price differentials could exist.

[2] R.C. Michie: "The London and New York Stock Exchanges 1850–1914," pp. 171–172.

> "However, all this was to change with the introduction of the telegraph in the mid-1840s, which provided for almost instantaneous communication between the different exchanges, and removed the barriers of distance that had preserved local markets."[3]

Though by 1852, the telegraph had become a reliable means of communication, costs of communicating with distant cities were still very high. Also, the longer the distance over which a message was transmitted, the lower was the level of accuracy of transmission of the message. The geographical areas whose cities' exchanges faced actual competition from New York, would, at first have included only cities that were in close physical proximity to New York; cities like Boston and Philadelphia. The "national" nature of the NYSE was limited to being a trans city exchange. Further improvements in the telegraph would have expanded the geographical area whose cities' exchanges faced competition from New York. And as Michie states, further developments in transport and communication would have expanded this geographical area. The NYSE would then have truly become a "national" exchange.

R.C. Michie has the right intuition, but he leaves the following questions unanswered: (i) when did the NYSE start becoming a "national" exchange, and (ii) why it was the NYSE and not exchanges at Philadelphia or Boston that became the "national" exchange. My research answers these questions.

Stock market data and the analyses of these data are necessary for deciding which of the many explanations propounded by economic logic and theory is correct.

For the dissertation on which this book is based, I collected and analyzed the data required to choose among these plausible causes. As this book works with data for the period, it can pinpoint the telegraph as the change in communications technology that led to the rise of NYSE to pre-eminence. Further changes such as the ticker tape and the telephone continued this process. In fact, the process continues today with the current enhancements in communications technology.

[3] R.C. Michie: "The London and New York Stock Exchanges 1850–1914," pp. 171–172.

References

Garbade, Kenneth D. and Silber, William L., "Technology, Communication and the Performance of Financial Markets: 1840–1975," *The Journal of Finance*. Vol. XXXIII, No. 3, June 1978.

DuBoff, R. B., "The Telegraph and the Structure of Markets in the United States, 1845–1890," *Research in Economic History*, Vol. 8, 1983, pp. 253–277.

CHAPTER 6

Data as Clues

Abstract Details of the data collected and the reasons why these data were collected are presented. Data are for the New York Stock Exchange, the Philadelphia Stock Exchange, and the Boston Stock Exchange for the years 1830–1860. Data are from contemporary newspapers from 1830 to 1860. Data on the Price and the Volume of securities traded are collected. Data on the Bid and Ask Prices of securities are also collected. Literature review on the relationship between volume of trade and bid ask spreads is included. Details of the frequency of reporting, the methodology for calculating the size of an exchange, the methodology for calculating average bid ask spreads, and the sampling procedure used are explained.

Keywords Average bid ask spreads · Bid ask spreads · Contemporary newspapers · Data source, characteristics, and description · Economies of scale · Liquidity · Price and Volume of securities traded · Price movement against the entity initiating the trade · Sampling procedure · Time needed to execute a trade · Boston public library · Boston stock exchange · Free library of Philadelphia · New York public library · NYSE and Philadelphia stock exchange

S. Garg, *The Telegraph and Stock Exchanges*, Palgrave Studies in Economic History, https://doi.org/10.1007/978-3-031-40407-8_6

The dissertation on which this book is based analyzes the price, quantity traded, and bid ask spreads for securities on the NYSE, the Philadelphia Stock Exchange, and the Boston Stock Exchange for the period 1835–1860. These data help us reconstruct what happened to market size and market efficiency during this period of structural change in securities markets.

What was Available Prior to this Book

The dissertation on which this book is based began with the desire to learn more about the history of stock exchanges during the period 1835–1860. There is no prior work on this period that used comprehensive stock market data.

Most historical work on US stock exchanges that used comprehensive data effectively began its analysis from either 1865 or 1880.

What this Book Contributes

The dissertation on which this book is based presents and analyzes stock market data for the period 1830–1860. For the first time, a picture is constructed of what happened to securities markets during this period. The analysis of this and supporting information proves that (i) the NYSE began its rise to pre-eminence in 1851–1852, and that this process accelerated post 1852; and (ii) that it was the telegraph becoming a reliable means of communication and being used to trade shares that caused this to happen.

Types of Data Collected and Analyzed

In order to figure out what happened, two sets of data are studied. The first is the price and volume data for securities traded on each of the exchanges. These data help to determine the relative size of each of the exchanges and to figure out movements in favor of or against exchanges.

The second is the bid and ask spread data for securities traded. One of the measures for efficiency of a stock transaction is the bid ask spread. These data help us compare the efficiency of exchanges, and discover if the most efficient exchange became the pre-eminent exchange.

An Explanation of Bid Ask Spreads

The bid price is the price at which the dealer or market maker will buy a share from an investor. The ask price is the price at which the dealer or market maker will sell the share to an investor. The difference between the two is the spread. The ask price is generally higher than the bid price The spread is a payment to the dealer or market maker for standing ready to buy when the investor wishes to sell, and standing ready to sell when the investor wishes to buy. In addition, the investor may have to incur costs such as commissions. *Ceteris paribus*, the lower the bid ask spread for a particular share or bond transaction, the lower the cost of doing business, and the more efficient the exchange. Another way of looking at the bid ask spread is to think of it as the cost of a round trip transaction, where you buy a security and sell it right back. Ignoring commissions for the moment, the cost of buying a security and selling it right back is the bid ask spread. For example, assume that for a security the bid price is $100.00 and the ask price is $100.25. You buy one share of the security and sell it right back. In this case you pay $100.25 to buy the security, and you receive $100.00 when you sell it right back. The cost to you of doing this is $100.25–$100.00 = $0.25 or the bid ask spread. For a single transaction such as a buy or a sell, half the bid ask spread is the cost. *Ceteris paribus*, the lower the bid ask spread for a security the lower the cost to an investor of trading in that security.

Bid Ask Spreads and Increases in Trading Volume

As the bid ask spread is a cost of doing business on an exchange, it is crucial to our understanding of competition between exchanges.

A stock exchange has economies of scale. This is so because a stock market has declining average costs over the relevant range of production. The costs of providing the service of trading stocks decline as more stocks are traded. Among the costs of trading a security are the following: (i) the time needed to execute a trade; (ii) the extent of price movement against the entity initiating the trade (in the event that the trade is executed); (iii) bid ask spread; and (iv) commissions. The first three typically go down as the number of shares of a particular security being traded increases.

As the number of shares traded of a particular stock rise, liquidity rises. As liquidity rises, we should expect the costs of transacting in that share to decline.

For any given trade that you wish to execute, the time needed to find someone with a matching trade reduces as liquidity increases, so that search time is reduced. The more buyers and sellers that get together to trade at a point, the more likely it is that a buyer or seller will find a matching trade. This reduces the time needed to execute a trade.

The market impact that your order has, i.e., how much you move the market price against yourself also decreases as liquidity increases, as your individual trade is now a smaller part of all stocks being traded.

The thicker the market i.e., the more shares being traded of a particular security, the less likely it is that a trade executed will move the market price against the entity executing the trade. In case the price does move against the entity initiating the trade this movement will tend to be smaller, the thicker the market.

The bid ask spread tends to decline as the number of securities traded at a particular venue increases. Buy and sell orders need not arrive at the same time. "The defining characteristic of a securities dealer is an affirmative obligation to trade with anyone who meets his price."[1] Thus, when you as an investor arrive at the market, wishing to execute a trade, you can either wait for someone with a matching trade, or you can trade with the dealer of that security. Securities dealers charge you for this service of standing willing to trade. One of the costs of trading with a dealer in securities is the bid ask spread. A dealer in securities will buy at a lower price (bid) and sell (ask) at a higher price. The difference is a payment for the provision of immediacy in executing your trade.

"Market makers play a central role in many equity markets by buying and selling shares to service the public's demand to trade immediately. Buyers and sellers arrive sporadically at the market, and it is not a simple matter for them to find each other in time. The market maker provides a solution by continuously standing ready to trade from his or her own inventory of shares. The service is not free; the dealer sells to buyers at higher ask prices, and buys from sellers at lower bid prices. The bid ask spread is the market maker's compensation (sometimes referred to as 'the dealer's turn')."[2]

[1] Treynor L. Jack, "dealers in securities" "*The New Palgrave Dictionary of Money and Finance*." Edited by, Peter Newman, Murray Millgate, and John Eatwell. 1992. Vol. (1).

[2] Shwartz, A. Robert, "market makers" *The New Palgrave Dictionary of Money and Finance*. Edited by, Peter Newman, Murray Millgate, and John Eatwell. 1992. Vol. (2).

Thus, the bid ask spread is compensation to the dealer in securities for providing an investor with immediacy, and it is a cost to the investor of transacting on the market. There are two costs the dealer incurs in order to provide investors with this service.

(a) He holds unwanted inventory. As the dealer trades at the time of others' choosing, he will be holding inventory he may not want for his investment purposes. He is investing his capital and must be compensated for this. In addition, he could have a long or a short position, which exposes him to risk.
(b) Trading with people more informed than himself. The securities dealer trades with two different types of people who wish to trade.

There are those who only have at best knowledge that is not private. They do not know more than the specialist knows. Among these are those that demand immediacy of execution and are willing to pay a price penalty, and those who are willing to wait till someone matches their price. The first kind is the ones that the dealer can charge a bid ask spread and make money from. There are also those who wish to trade for investment purposes, but are willing to wait till someone matches their price. Such people might have evaluated the value of the share, and wish to trade at that price.

The second kind of person is one that is more informed than the specialist. They are trading on information that the specialist does not have at the moment. The specialist cannot make money off such people and generally loses money when he trades with them. The dealer faces the risk that when trading with these people, he may be buying into a market that is falling, or selling into a market that is rising.

The dealer must be compensated for the costs and risks that he undertakes. The bid ask spread is one such compensation.

These costs and risks per transaction reduce as the number of securities being traded at a particular venue rise. Therefore, we would expect the bid ask spread to decline too.

Ceteris paribus, the costs of doing business for a dealer in securities decline, as the market becomes thicker. As more and more buy and sell orders arrive, the average time that a dealer has to hold an unwanted position declines. Therefore, if we are in a competitive environment, we would expect prices; in this case, the bid ask spreads to decline. Two papers, one by Demsetz (1968) and the other by Copeland and Galai (1983), find that for the sample of stocks and the period studied, bid ask spreads decline as volume traded increases.

Stock exchanges have declining average costs over the relevant range of output, i.e., they have economies of scale. This implies that trading in a particular security will concentrate at one exchange. In case that does happen, there is the possibility that monopoly prices will be charged, i.e., well above costs.

There are several factors that will prevent non-competitive prices from being charged. Though a stock exchange has the characteristics of a natural monopoly, the dealer in a security, for example in the case of NYSE, the specialist, is not a monopolist. He faces competition from several sources.

According to Harold Demsetz, "*The Cost of Transacting*" Quarterly Journal of Economics, 1968 "Even though scale economies are present in the specialist's trading activities, there is little likelihood of his maintaining spread much above the cost of waiting. Competition of several types will keep the observed spread close to cost. The main types of competition emanate from (1) rivalry for the specialist's job, (2) competing markets, (3) outsiders who submit limit orders, (4) floor traders who may bypass the floor specialist by crossing buy and sell orders themselves, and (5) other specialists."[3] (Demsetz 1968).

We would expect price to be close to average costs. Thus, bid ask spreads should decline as volume increases.

Description of Data Sources

The dissertation on which this book is based uses contemporary newspapers to recover the pertinent data. The process took several months with various false leads. One of the first places searched was the Hunt's Merchant Magazine, as it was considered the primary source for historical data on securities. Hunt's Merchant Magazine reported only the highest and the lowest security prices for the period under review.

The Smithsonian Museum was visited in the search for data. The data being sought were not there.

[3] Demsetz, Harold, "The Cost of Transacting" *Quarterly Journal of Economics, 1968.*
Copeland, E. Thomas and Galai, Dan, "*Information Effects on the Bid-Ask Spread,*" *Journal of Finance 38 (December 1983).*

The next source investigated was the archives of the NYSE. The archives had incomplete records.

The New York Public Library was the next stop. Here a search of contemporary newspapers revealed the bid price and ask price data. These were reported weekly or bimonthly. The price and volume data were reported daily.

In order to get the data for Boston, a search was made of newspapers at the Boston Public Library. The data were spread over several journals, changing titles often. However, even though the newspapers and journals in which the data were reported changed often, the data reporting was continuous and consistent. In several instances, when the data moved from one newspaper to another, the same template was used in the new newspaper. Usually, not more than one newspaper reported the data at a time; the reporting was transferred from one newspaper to another. The only time two newspapers reported the data at the same time, the data were identical.

For Philadelphia, a search was conducted at the Free Library of Philadelphia. Newspapers from the 1830s to the 1860s had bid ask spread data for the Philadelphia Stock Exchange.

Copies of the relevant newspapers from all three libraries were available on microfilm. I took printouts of the relevant pages from the microfilms. The data on these printouts were then manually entered into a computer.

Table 6.1 contains a brief description of data sources.

Description of Data

The data used in this book are derived from microfilm copies of contemporary newspaper sources for the period 1830–1862. Two types of data are used. Price and volume data, and bid ask spread data. For both sets of data, the data for the last recorded day of the month are used. After making photocopies of the newspapers, these data were entered manually onto a computer.

There was often trading on a second board for Boston, Philadelphia, and New York. The total for the day includes all trading on an exchange on a particular day.

Data on bid ask spreads in Boston for securities were reported and divided into categories such as Government Securities, City Securities, Railroad Bonds, Banks, Insurance Companies, Railroad, Manufactories, Copper Mining Companies, and Miscellaneous.

Table 6.1 Data sources, characteristics, and description

Number of Cities: 3			
Names of Cities	New York	Philadelphia	Boston
Price & Volume data available	1830–1832, 1834–1865	1832–1851	1835, 1836, 1839, 1840, 1843–1862
Bid Ask Spread data available	1830–1832, 1834–1851	1832–1835, 1838–1856, 1860	1835, 1836,1844–1862
Frequency of data available			
Price, Volume	Daily		
Bid Ask spread	weekly-bimonthly		
Frequency of data used in computations			
Price data	Monthly	Last reported day of the month	
Number of shares traded	Monthly	Last reported day of the month	
Bid ask spread	Monthly	Last reported day of the month	
Newspapers: New York Journal of Commerce and Commercial, New York' New York Journal of Commerce; Weekly Journal of Commerce			
Newspapers: Boston The Boston Atlas; Evening Mercantile Journal; Columbian Cenitel; The Daily Atlas; Boston Shipping List; The Daily Bee; The Boston Daily Bee; The Daily Evening Bee; Boston Atlas and Bee Boston; The Commercial Bulletin; Boston Atlas and Bee; Daily Evening Traveller; Boston Daily Traveller; Boston Daily Evening Traveller			
Newspapers: Philadelphia Bicknell's Reporter, Counterfeit Detector and Prices Current; Bicknell's Reporter, Counterfeit Detector and Philadelphia Prices Current; Philadelphia Commercial List and Price Current; Sunday Dispatch; Philadelphia Press			

Data on bid ask spreads in Philadelphia for securities were reported and divided into categories such as Loans, Bank Stocks, Insurance Stocks, Canal Stocks, Railroad Stocks, and Miscellaneous Stocks.

Data on bid ask spreads in New York for securities were reported and divided into categories such as Public Securities, Banks, Marine Insurance, Fire Insurance, Joint Stock Companies, Exchange (this referred to other exchanges such as those in Amsterdam and France), and Gold and Silver (These were the categories in 1830). The categories in 1841 were Stocks, Banks, Banking Associations, Trust Companies, Foreign Institutions (these were institutions from other parts of the country such as United States Bank, Illinois State Bank, Louisiana Bank, and Bank of Kentucky), Marine Insurance, Fire Insurance, Miscellaneous, Railroads, and Specie. The categories in 1851 were Government Securities, State Securities, City and Co., Banks, Trust Companies, Foreign Institutions (United States Bank, Louisiana Bank, and Illinois State Bank), Marine Insurance, Fire Insurance Companies, Miscellaneous, Railroads, and Bonds.

For price and volume of securities traded, the following are recorded. For bonds traded, the following are recorded in the newspapers:

> The total dollar value of the transaction at maturity is in the first column of the records. The name and description of the bond are recorded in the second column. The price per unit at which the trade took place is recorded in the third column. For bonds the total face value at maturity of a particular transaction, and the price at which this trade took place is recorded, for example, $ 1,000 of Illinois 6 per cents at $ 51.50 on February 27, 1841, in New York.

For shares traded, the following are recorded:

> The number of shares traded is recorded in the left-hand or first column. The name of the security is recorded in the middle or second column. The price per share at which the trade took place is recorded in the right hand or third column. For shares traded, the number of shares and the price at which the transaction took place is recorded. For example, 35 shares of the Bank of Commerce were recorded as being traded at a price of $ 94.75 per share on February 27, 1841, in New York.

The newspapers reported each transaction that took place on a particular day, i.e., the individual transactions that took place are recorded. No aggregate figure for the day's transactions exists. The record provides a wealth of detail such as the total number of transactions, the total number of securities traded, the total number of transactions in each security, the size of each transaction, and the price at which each transaction occurred. This wealth of detail is used later in the book for analyzing the movement of trades in Reading Railroad from the Philadelphia Stock Exchange to the NYSE. This wealth of detail led to the first order of business when it came to comparing the size of each exchange; to wit, that of aggregation. This is dealt with in the next section.

For each of the exchanges, data on the price and volume of securities traded are available on a daily frequency and are reported for each day (except for Philadelphia during the periods August 1832–March 1833, June 1835–September 1835, February 1841–August 1842, November 1842–March 1843, and August 1843–September 1843, when they are reported as aggregated by week). Data are available for Monday through Saturday.

For the bid and ask data, the following are recorded:

> The names of all securities that could be traded on that exchange are listed. This is unlike for the price and volume data, where the only securities that are mentioned on a particular day are the ones that were traded on that day. For bid ask spreads, a template is used by the newspapers.

For the NYSE, the name of the security is recorded in the left-hand or first column. The bid (what the dealer in the security is bidding for the security) or the price at which an investor could sell the security is recorded in the middle or second column. The ask (what the dealer in the security is asking for the security) or the price at which an investor could buy the security is recorded in the right hand or third column. There are numerous instances when either a bid, an ask or both are not reported for a particular security.

For Philadelphia and Boston, for several of the years under consideration, there are five things recorded. The name of the security is recorded in the first column. The par value of the security is recorded in the second column. The bid or offered price is recorded in the third column. The ask price is recorded in the fourth column, and remarks relating to dividends are recorded in the fifth column. For several of the years under consideration, the par value is not reported for Philadelphia and Boston.

An example of the bid ask spread: For the Philadelphia Stock Exchange, on January 24, 1853, for the Bank of the United States an offer or bid price of $3.50 and an ask price of $4.00 are recorded.

For each of the exchanges, the data are available at least on a bimonthly frequency, and in most cases are available on a weekly basis. For many of the years under review, Philadelphia and New York had a biweekly reporting frequency.

Methodology for Calculating the Size of Each Exchange

In order to aggregate for the volume or number of shares and bonds traded each day, the data on the number of bonds traded had to be extracted from the total face value at maturity for bonds. Given the available information, this is not possible, as we do not know the dollar denomination of each individual bond. For bonds, we have only the face value at maturity of each transaction from which we cannot extract the total number of bonds traded.

We have the total number of shares traded.

As we do not know the total number of bonds traded, we cannot calculate the aggregate volume of trade, i.e., calculate the total number of shares and bonds traded on a particular day.

Comparing just the total number of shares traded presents another problem. At the time, the possible range of par value was very large, as the par value of securities was not standardized. To aggregate the volume for shares with different par values presents a problem. For example, we could have one exchange where 500 shares of par value $100 each, and price $80 were traded on a particular day, and another exchange where 500 shares of par value $1000 each, and price $800 were traded. Comparing volumes would give us a figure of 500 shares for each exchange, although the second exchange is larger than the first. Consequently, the volume of trade is not calculated.

The value of trade on a particular day is calculated in the following way.

For shares, the number of shares traded is multiplied by the price, to give the value of the transaction. For bonds, the face value at maturity of each transaction is taken as the value of the transaction. The values of all share and bond transactions for a particular day are added to give the aggregate value of trade for that particular day.

Methodology for Calculating the Average Bid Ask Spread for an Exchange

To calculate the average bid ask spreads for an exchange the following is done: For each day, the securities considered are those for which both the bid and the ask price are recorded. Average bid ask spreads are calculated as follows. For an individual security, the difference between bid and ask price is taken. This constitutes the numerator. The average of the bid and ask price is the denominator. The result of this fraction is recorded for an individual security. The results for all the securities for that day are then averaged to get the average spread on a particular day, for an exchange.

Sampling Procedure

For each month in the period 1830–1860 for which data were available, the last reported day of the month is used. The aggregate value of trade for this day is taken as a proxy for the month. Taking the last reported day's data as a proxy for the month is standard procedure in finance literature. Three experts in the field, Prof. Richard Sylla at the Stern School of Management at New York University, Dr. Tim Opler at the WR Hambrecht + Co. in New York, and Prof. Charles Calomiris at Columbia University in New York were consulted and all three agreed on the appropriateness of the sampling procedure.

This sampling procedure helped save considerable time, as it took on average 5 man-hours to calculate the aggregate value of trade for one day. The extent of data that were entered onto a computer for purposes of analysis for this dissertation is as follows: 391 months for New York i.e., 32 years and 7 months (original data considered for New York ran from 1830–1865), 298 months for Philadelphia i.e., 24 years and 10 months, and 241 months for Boston, i.e., 20 years and 1 month. Price and volume data are reported for all days except Sunday, i.e., for each year for (365–52) days.

For New York, data for 391 days were collected and converted to electronic formats. Had this sampling not been done, data for (365–52) × 32 + [(7 × 30)-30 days i.e., 10,196 days would have had to be collected and converted. As this was done for only 391 data days, instead of for 10,196, the time required to record data for 10,196–391 days = 9805 days was saved. As each day took 5 man-hours to record, my sampling procedure saved me 49,025 man-hours. Similarly, for Philadelphia without the sampling procedure, there would have been a need to convert data for (365–52) × 24 + [(10 × 30)–43] = 7769 days. Using the sampling data for only 298 days saved the time required to convert data for 7769–298 = 7471 days, which translates into 37,355 man-hours. For Boston, without the sampling procedure, there would have been a need to convert data for (365–52) × 20 + [(1 × 30)-4] = 6286 days. Using the sampling procedure, data for only 241 days was converted, saving the time required to convert data for 6286–241 = 6045 days. That translates into 30,225 man-hours. Thus, the sampling procedure allowed conversion to be done in only 4650 man-hours instead of 121,255 man-hours, saving 116,605 man-hours. Bid ask spread data were also recorded just once a month for similar reasons.

References

Copeland, E. Thomas and Galai, Dan, "Information Effects on the Bid-Ask Spread," *Journal of Finance*, Vol. 38, December 1983.

Demsetz, Harold, "The Cost of Transacting," *Quarterly Journal of Economics* (1968).

CHAPTER 7

When: The Numbers Through a Telescope

Abstract The data on the value of securities traded are graphed and analyzed to establish when the New York Stock Exchange began its rise to pre-eminence. Data for value of securities traded are presented as graphs. Value of securities traded = (Price of Security × Number of securities sold) + (face value at maturity of bonds). For the New York Stock Exchange: 12 data points for each year; one for each month. Similarly for the Philadelphia Stock Exchange and the Boston Stock Exchange. Graph 7.1 has data from 1835 to 1863. Graph 7.2 has data from 1835 to 1854 and Graph 7.3 has data from 1844 to 1852. Graph 7.4 presents 60 month moving average of the value of securities traded data. Analysis of graphs shows that the NYSE began its rise to pre-eminence in 1851–1852, and this process accelerated post 1852.

Keywords Value of securities traded · NYSE's rise to pre-eminence · NYSE began its rise to pre-eminence in 1851–1852 · Process (of the NYSE's rise to pre-eminence) escalated substantially after 1852 · Telegraph became a reliable means of communication (1852)

S. Garg, *The Telegraph and Stock Exchanges*, Palgrave Studies in Economic History, https://doi.org/10.1007/978-3-031-40407-8_7

The data on the value of securities traded from 1835 to 1863 are graphed and analyzed to establish when the NYSE began its rise to pre-eminence.

Explanation of Graphs Depicting Size of Each Exchange

The graphs are constructed as follows. The X-axis records time. Data for each of the 12 months of a year are recorded. There are 12 entries for each year. For each month of a particular year, the year itself is recorded. The Y-axis shows the value of securities traded. There are three series corresponding to each of the three exchanges.

Graph 7.1 is for data from 1835 to 1863. Graph 7.2 is for data from 1835 to 1854. Graph 7.3 is for data from 1844 to 1852. Graph 7.4 depicts 60 month moving averages for data from 1835 to 1862. Data; in Excel, for these graphs is in Appendix A.

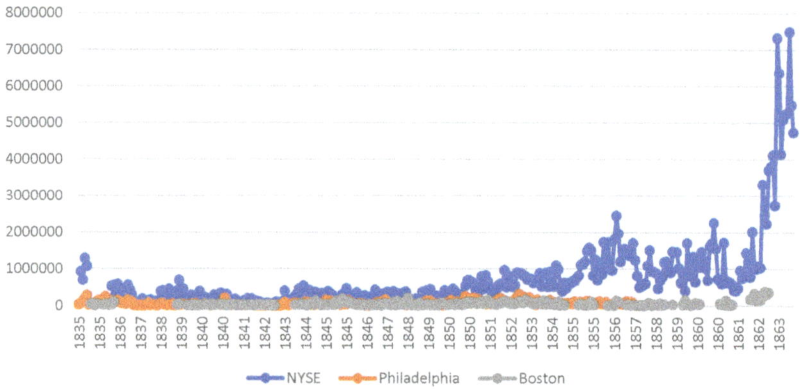

Graph 7.1 Value of securities traded (in $ [USD]). 1835–1863

Graph 7.2 looks at part of the data in more detail than Graph 7.1.

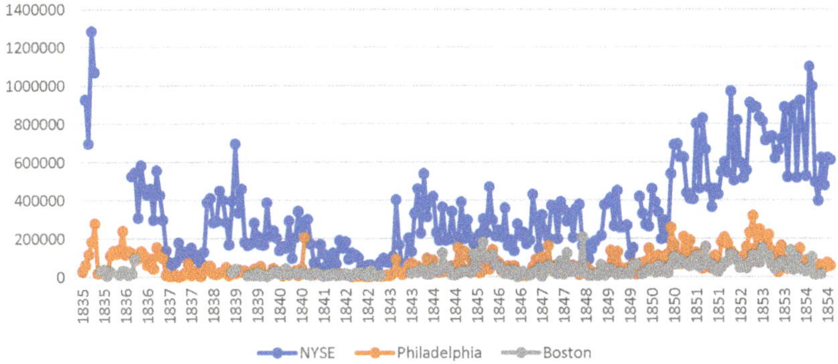

Graph 7.2 Value of securities traded (in $ [USD]). 1835–1854

The period 1844 to 1852 is studied in more detail using Graph 7.3; from the advent of the telegraph (1844) to its becoming a reliable means of communication (1852).

Graph 7.1 shows the phenomenal rise of the NYSE after 1852. It shows that though the NYSE was typically larger than the other two exchanges prior to 1851–1852,[1] this was trifling compared to its absolute

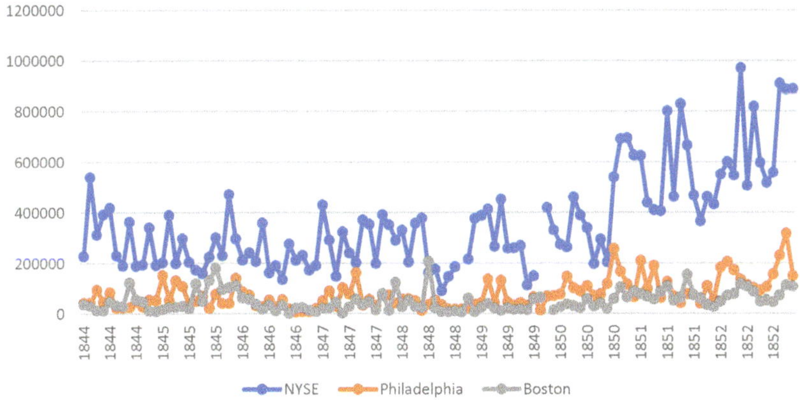

Graph 7.3 Value of securities traded (in $ [USD]). 1844–1852

[1] On May 31, 1848, the value of securities traded on the Boston Stock Exchange was greater than the value of securities traded on the NYSE, and on the Philadelphia Exchange.

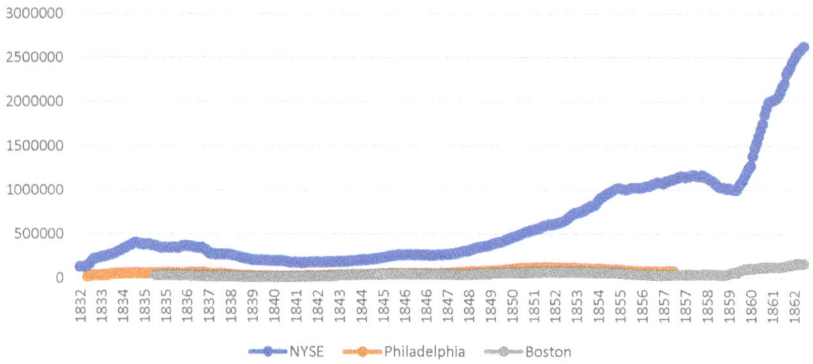

Graph 7.4 Value of securities traded (in $ [USD]). (1832–1862) 60 month (5 year) moving average

and relative size after 1852. Graph 7.2 shows what happened between 1835 and 1854 in greater detail than does Graph 7.1. Graph 7.2 is constructed to show the period 1835–1854 in detail. Graph 7.2 gives a detailed view of part of the period in question, and Graph 7.1 gives an overall view of the entire period. Each helps illustrate a point. Graph 7.2 illustrates the competition among the three exchanges prior to 1851–1852, and Graph 7.1 illustrates the absolute lack of it after 1852. Graph 7.3 is a detailed view of the period 1844 to 1852: the period from the advent of the telegraph, to it becoming a reliable means of communication.

Results from Analyzing the Graphs on Size of Exchanges

The results are as follows: Up until 1850, though the NYSE was typically larger than the other two,[2] the differences in their relative sizes were much smaller in this period as compared to the differences in their relative sizes post 1852.

[2] On May 31, 1848, the value of securities traded on the Boston Stock Exchange was greater than the value of securities traded on the NYSE, and on the Philadelphia Exchange.

It was not until 1851–1852 that the NYSE began its rise to pre-eminence, and the process accelerated post 1852. Several times before 1851–1852, the NYSE was substantially larger than the other two exchanges, but then it came down to being close in size to the other two again. The NYSE was significantly larger than the other two exchanges for one month in 1832, several months in 1834, four months in 1835 (this particular time it was trading in just four types of railway bonds that contributed the majority of value), and several months in 1844 and 1849. The difference between the NYSE and the other two exchanges increased substantially after 1852.

These graphs reveal that the NYSE began its rise to pre-eminence in 1851–1852 and that this process escalated substantially after 1852.

Chapter 8 explains why this happened.

CHAPTER 8

Why: The Numbers Under a Magnifying Glass

Abstract Each of the reasons for the rise of the NYSE to pre-eminence posited earlier is discussed in light of what the value of securities traded graphs reveal; (i) that the NYSE began its rise to pre-eminence in 1851–1852, and (ii) that this process accelerated after 1852. The chapter also analyzes the explanations for the NYSE launching into prominence presented in other resources: Erie Canal, Population, Wealth, and Stock Ticker. The plausible causes for the rise of the New York Stock Exchange to pre-eminence are examined based on the data. (i) Population (ii) Wealth (iii) Opening of the Erie Canal and the (iv) Stock Ticker are analyzed as well as market efficiency.

Keywords Average bid ask spreads · Consolidated Stock Exchange of New York (Consolidated) · Erie Canal · Large size, medium size, and small size trade · Most efficient exchange · Population · Reading Railroad · Stock ticker · Telegraph · Wealth

S. Garg, *The Telegraph and Stock Exchanges*, Palgrave Studies in Economic History, https://doi.org/10.1007/978-3-031-40407-8_8

The Telegraph, With the Bid Ask Spread, in New York

Evaluating the Hypotheses

Each possible reason for the rise of the NYSE to pre-eminence posited earlier is discussed in light of what the value of securities traded graphs reveal; (i) the NYSE began its rise to pre-eminence in 1851–1852, and (ii) that this process accelerated after 1852.

Eliminating Hypotheses That Fail

Erie Canal

The Erie Canal opened in 1825. Graphs 7.1, 7.2, and 7.3 show that the significant shift in the total value of securities traded in favor of the NYSE was not until after 1851–1852, more than a quarter of a century after the opening of the Erie Canal. Thus, the Erie Canal was not the immediate cause of the rise of the NYSE to pre-eminence.

The larger size of the NYSE prior to 1851–1852 could be attributed in part to the increased economic activity in New York because of the Erie Canal. As this larger size relative to the other two exchanges gave the NYSE an edge when the exchanges began competing, the opening of the Erie Canal contributed to the rise of the NYSE to pre-eminence in the future. Had a technological innovation like the telegraph not connected the three cities and provided a reliable means of communicating between these cities in real time, the NYSE would have remained larger than the other two exchanges, without becoming the pre-eminent exchange.

Population

Table 8.1 and Graph 8.1 contain population data for each city. These are reported by decade, and census data are used. As census data are reported every ten years, these data have been interpolated over the intervening years, taking an equal rise in population in each year for which data are not reported.

Graph 8.1 shows that New York had the largest population among the three cities long before 1851–1852. Thus, population was not the reason the NYSE rose to pre-eminence. If the population of New York City was the reason that the NYSE rose to pre-eminence, then the NYSE should have risen to pre-eminence long before 1851–1852.

Table 8.1 City population (1820–1870)

Population			
Year	*City*		
	New York City	*Philadelphia*	*Boston*
1820	123,706	63,802	43,298
1830	202,589	80,462	61,392
1840	312,710	93,665	93,385
1850	515,547	121,376	136,881
1860	813,669	565,529	177,840
1870	942,292	674,022	250,526

Source US Census. 1820–1860

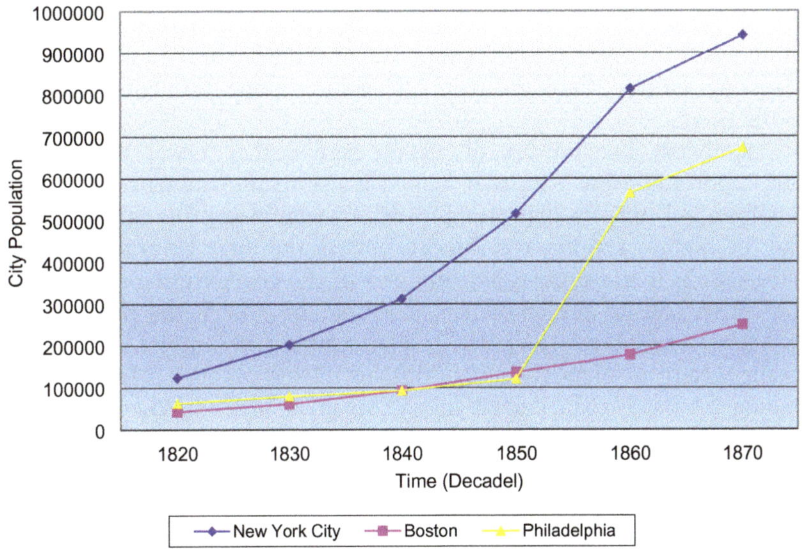

Graph 8.1 City population (1820–1870)

Imports and Exports

Table 8.2 and Graph 8.2 contain import and export data (Data are by state). Data on imports and exports are used in lieu of data on wealth, and as an indicator of the level of economic activity for each city, in part because I was unable to get comparable data for the wealth of each city for the entire period under study.

Annual data on wealth are available for New York, and data on Boston are available only by decade, but no comparable data exist for Philadelphia. Annual data on imports and exports for each city are available for all years except 1854 and 1855. There is a high correlation (0.86) between the wealth and the sum of exports and imports for New York City. Thus, the sum of exports and imports is used in lieu of wealth data. There are two different sources for data on exports and imports of the three cities. For data up to 1853, the source is the compendium to the 1850 US Census, published in 1856. For data from 1856 onwards, the source is the Statistical Abstract of the United States, published in 1879. This is under the First session of the 46th Congress of the House of Representatives meeting in 1878 and is included in the report on "Finance, Coinage, Commerce, Immigration, Shipping, The Postal Service, Population, Railroads, Agriculture, Coal and Iron." There are three series, corresponding to the three cities.

The theory that we are discussing here is that it was the exports and imports of New York that helped it rise to pre-eminence. A glance at Graph 8.2 reveals that this theory is the wrong one, as New York had the highest exports and imports among the three cities long before 1851–1852. If the exports and imports of the city were the reason that the NYSE rose to pre-eminence, it should have been the pre-eminent exchange long before 1851–1852. The exports and imports contributed to the wealth of New York, and this, to the extent that it led to more trading on the NYSE, helped the NYSE grow in size. When the three exchanges began competing with each other, the NYSE's size relative to the other two exchanges gave it an advantage that led to its rise to pre-eminence. Exports, imports, and the wealth of the city before 1851–1852 contributed to the rise of the NYSE to pre-eminence in the future. Had a technological innovation like the telegraph not connected the three cities and provided a reliable means of communicating between these cities in real time, the NYSE would have remained larger than the other two exchanges, without becoming the pre-eminent exchange.

Stock Ticker

The stock ticker was introduced in 1867, long after our data show that the NYSE emerged as the pre-eminent exchange. Thus, the stock ticker was not the reason the NYSE rose to pre-eminence, as it was introduced

Table 8.2 Value of exports and imports

State-wise commerce							
Imports				*Exports*			
Year	*New York*	*Pennsylvania*	*Massachusetts*	*Year*	*New York*	*Pennsylvania*	*Massachusetts*
1821	23,629,246	8,158,922	14,826,732	1821	13,162,917	7,391,767	12,484,691
1822	35,445,628	11,874,170	18,337,320	1822	17,100,482	9,047,802	12,598,525
1823	29,421,349	13,696,770	17,607,160	1823	19,038,990	9,617,192	13,683,239
1824	36,113,723	11,865,531	15,378,758	1824	22,897,134	9,364,893	10,434,328
1825	49,639,174	15,041,797	15,848,141	1825	35,259,261	11,269,981	11,432,987
1826	38,115,630	13,551,779	17,063,482	1826	21,947,791	8,331,722	10,098,862
1827	38,719,644	11,212,935	13,370,564	1827	23,834,137	7,575,833	10,424,383
1828	41,927,792	12,884,408	15,070,444	1828	22,777,649	6,051,480	9,025,785
1829	34,743,307	10,100,152	12,520,744	1829	20,119,011	4,089,935	8,254,937
1830	35,624,070	8,702,122	10,453,544	1830	19,697,983	4,291,793	7,213,194
1831	57,077,417	12,124,083	14,269,056	1831	25,535,144	5,513,713	7,733,763
1832	53,214,402	10,678,358	18,118,900	1832	26,000,945	3,516,066	11,993,768
1833	55,918,449	10,451,250	19,940,911	1833	25,395,117	4,078,951	9,683,122
1834	73,188,594	10,479,268	17,672,129	1834	25,512,014	3,989,746	10,148,820
1835	88,191,305	12,389,937	19,800,373	1835	30,345,264	3,739,275	10,043,790
1836	118,253,416	15,068,233	25,681,462	1836	28,920,438	3,971,555	10,384,346
1837	79,301,722	11,680,111	19,975,667	1837	27,338,419	3,841,599	9,728,190
1838	68,453,206	9,360,371	13,300,925	1838	23,008,471	3,477,151	9,104,862
1839	99,882,438	15,050,715	19,385,223	1839	33,268,099	5,255,415	9,276,085
1840	60,440,750	8,469,882	16,513,858	1840	34,264,080	6,820,145	10,186,261
1841	75,713,426	10,346,698	20,318,003	1841	33,139,833	5,152,501	11,487,343
1842	55,875,604	7,385,758	17,986,433	1842	27,576,778	3,776,727	9,807,116

(continued)

Table 8.2 (continued)

State-wise commerce

Imports				*Exports*			
Year	*New York*	*Pennsylvania*	*Massachusetts*	*Year*	*New York*	*Pennsylvania*	*Massachusetts*
1843	31,356,540	2,760,630	16,789,452	1843	13,443,234	2,071,945	4,431,681
1844	65,079,510	7,217,267	20,296,087	1844	32,861,540	3,535,256	9,096,286
1845	70,909,085	8,159,227	22,781,024	1845	36,175,298	3,574,363	10,351,030
1846	74,254,283	7,989,396	24,190,963	1846	36,935,413	4,751,005	10,313,118
1847	84,167,352	9,587,516	34,477,008	1847	49,844,368	8,544,391	11,248,462
1848	94,525,141	12,147,584	28,647,707	1848	53,351,157	5,732,333	13,419,699
1849	92,567,369	10,645,500	24,745,917	1849	45,963,100	5,343,421	10,264,862
1850	111,123,524	12,066,154	30,374,684	1850	52,712,789	4,501,606	10,681,763
1851	141,546,538	14,168,761	32,715,327	1851	86,007,019	5,356,036	12,352,682
1852	132,329,306	14,785,917	33,504,789	1852	87,484,456	5,828,571	16,546,499
1853	178,270,999	18,834,410	41,367,956	1853	66,030,355	6,255,229	16,895,304
1854	189,379,211	16,054,464	40,326,711	1854	88,804,706	6,050,479	23,700,313
1855	162,583,119	13,782,848	34,620,709	1855	88,246,295	6,012,434	23,551,284
1856	195,645,515	16,585,685	41,661,068	1856	104,861,799	7,144,488	27,985,651
1857	222,550,307	17,850,630	44,840,083	1857	124,389,467	7,135,156	28,326,918
1858	170,280,887	12,890,369	40,432,710	1858	100,702,661	5,987,251	20,979,853
1859	218,231,093	14,517,542	41,174,670	1859	106,478,429	5,345,105	16,172,120
1860	233,692,941	14,626,801	39,366,560	1860	138,145,644	5,598,267	15,168,015
1861	222,966,274	12,625,448	44,014,151	1861	150,691,451	9,975,078	15,448,464

State-wise commerce

Imports				*Exports*			
Year	*New York*	*Pennsylvania*	*Massachusetts*	*Year*	*New York*	*Pennsylvania*	*Massachusetts*
1862	142,215,636	5,817,190	23,957,621	1862	162,780,045	11,082,119	13,871,135
1863	177,254,415	7,392,785	27,083,272	1863	239,287,331	12,268,675	21,354,061
1864	229,506,499	9,141,672	30,263,853	1864	223,972,862	10,212,700	16,625,110
1865	154,139,409	7,319,520	24,540,494	1865	242,006,891	11,053,465	21,428,641

First session of the 46th Congress of the House of Representatives meeting in 1878
The report on "Finance, Coinage, Commerce, Immigration, Shipping, The Postal Service, Population"
New York City is in the state of New York. Philadelphia City is in the state of Pennsylvania. Boston City is in the state of Massachusetts
Sources
For data up to 1853. The Compendium to the 1850 US Census. Published 1856
For data from 1856 onwards. The Statistical Abstract of the United States. Published in 1879

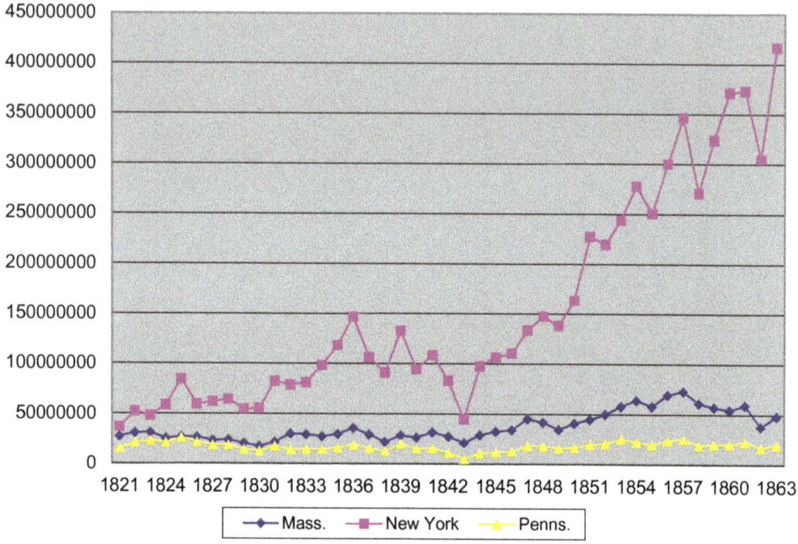

Graph 8.2 Exports + Imports ($) 1821–1863. State-wise data

a decade and a half after the NYSE rose to pre-eminence. Though the stock ticker was not the cause of the rise of the NYSE to pre-eminence, it continued the trend started by the telegraph by further reducing the cost of disseminating information. The stock ticker was one in a line of innovations in communications technology that started with the introduction of the telegraph, and its use led to even more trade being conducted through the NYSE.

The Most Probable Hypothesis

Telegraph

Given the timing of the rise of the NYSE, the telegraph seemed the most likely cause for the rise of the NYSE to pre-eminence. However, there was a problem. New York City, Philadelphia, and Boston were linked by telegraph lines by 1846. Why did it take till 1851–1852 for the NYSE to begin its rise to pre-eminence? Fellow economic history students at the Economics Department at The Ohio State University rallied round to help answer this question. Someone said that it takes seven years for a new technology to be adopted. Others agreed and added that that is what they had heard. Some suggested that as people are resistant to new technology, it takes time for a new technology to be adopted. People are typically resistant to new technology. On the other hand, a new technology that helps you make money is often adopted quickly. Even if one accepted that new technology took time to be adopted, why would seven years be the magic number? Why not six years, or eight years? An answer with a more concrete base was required.

After several months of reading and several discussions, I came upon Tomas Nonnenmacher's PhD thesis,[1] which talked about the fact that it took time for the telegraph to become a reliable means of communication, and lo and behold, the fact that the telegraph became a reliable means of communication by 1852. This dissertation provided all the proof needed. Or did it?

The next question that was posed was: even though the telegraph became a reliable means of communication by 1852, was it being used to trade securities? Proof of this was required. I was at a loss, wondering how to get proof of something that may or may not have occurred in 1852. Would someone have even recorded such information at the time; and if they had, would it be available now? And if it was available, how to find this information? Another six months passed, till I came across mention of a survey[2] submitted in 1852, which provided proof that the telegraph was being used to trade securities in 1851, and that though the reliability of the telegraph had vastly improved by 1851, there were still some issues with the telegraph's reliability.

Tomas Nonnenmacher's PhD dissertation[3] and the survey[4] submitted in 1852 helped establish the fact that the use of the telegraph to trade securities, brought the three exchanges into competition with each other.

[1] Nonnenmacher, Tomas W., "Law, Emerging Technology, and Market Structure: The Development of the Telegraph Industry, 1838–1868." *Ph.D. Dissertation*. 1995.

[2] Survey included in the book: Jones, Alexander "Historical Sketch of the Electric Telegraph: Including Its Rise and Progress in the United States." George P. Putnam, 10 Park Place, New York. 1852.

[3] Nonnenmacher, Tomas W., "Law, Emerging Technology, and Market Structure: The Development of the Telegraph Industry, 1838–1868." *Ph.D. Dissertation*. 1995.

[4] Survey included in the book: Jones, Alexander, "Historical Sketch of the Electric Telegraph: Including Its Rise and Progress in the United States." George P. Putnam, 10 Park Place, New York. 1852.

The next question that arose was: why it was the NYSE and not the other two exchanges that emerged as the winners of this competition? This question is answered below.

The telegraph was invented and effectively demonstrated in 1844. Two years later, telegraph lines were being installed between major cities.

Table 8.3 reproduces Table 2.1 from Tomas Nonnenmacher's PhD dissertation[5] and shows the dissemination of the telegraph by listing the number of telegraph lines installed and the capital invested in each of the lines from 1846 to 1860. This table shows the spread and dissemination of the telegraph and lets us know when each of the major cities was linked by the telegraph.

Table 8.3 shows the development of Telegraph lines in the early years.

New York City emerged as the most widely connected city early on in the development of the system.

Initially, the telegraph was not a reliable means of communication.

Messages were often garbled. Telegraph lines were improperly insulated. There were gradual improvements in telegraph technology.

In addition, it took time to train telegraph operators.

Several other aspects relating to the telegraph took time to perfect, such as property rights relating to the messages sent; priority ranking when it came to sending messages; and methods for assigning responsibility and punishments when messages were incorrectly sent or incorrectly delivered.

The telegraph became a reliable means of communication by 1852. This is established in "Law, Emerging Technology, and Market Structure: The Development of the Telegraph Industry, 1838–1868," by Tomas Nonnenmacher (Ph.D. Dissertation).

Though telegraph lines between major cities were operational by 1846, it took till 1852 for the telegraph to become a reliable means of communication.

By 1851–1852, the three exchanges were competing with each other. Investors could choose which venue to trade at. Why was it the NYSE and not one of the other two exchanges that emerged as the winner of this competition?

Given a choice of stock exchanges to trade at, *ceteris paribus*, investors will choose to trade on the most efficient exchange, one that *inter alia*,

[5] Nonnenmacher, Tomas W. "Law, Emerging Technology, and Market Structure: The Development of the Telegraph Industry, 1838–1868." *Ph.D. Dissertation*. 1995.

Table 8.3 Entry and exit of major Telegraph lines

Date	*Name*	*Location*	*Original promoter*	*State of Incorp.*	*Original capital*	*Patent*
1/27/46	Magnetic Telegraph Corporation	New York, Philadelphia, and Washington	Morse	Maryland	$60,000	Morse
6/27/46	New York and Boston Magnetic Telegraph Company	New York and Boston	Smith	Mass. & Conn	$160,000	Morse
11/2/46	Washington and New Orleans Telegraph Co	New York and New Orleans	Morse	Alabama, North Carolina	$561,700	Morse
1846	New York, Albany, and Buffalo Telegraph Company	New York and Buffalo	Morse	New York	$200,000	Morse
12/26/46	Atlantic and Ohio Telegraph Company	Philadelphia and Pittsburgh	O'Rielly	Penn	$300,000	Morse/ Pirate
8/20/47	Pittsburgh, Cincinnati and, Louisville Telegraph Company	Pittsburgh and Louisville	O'Rielly	Indiana	$138,000	Morse/ Pirate/ Bain
12/10/47	Ohio and Mississippi Telegraph Company	Louisville and St. Louis	O'Rielly	Indiana	$200,000	Morse/ Pirate/ Bain
11/20/47–5/ 48	Lake Erie Telegraph Company	Buffalo, Detroit, and Milwaukee	O'Rielly	New York		Morse/ Pirate/ Bain
2/28/48	New York and Erie Telegraph Company	New York and Buffalo	Smith	New York	Estimated at $34,880	Morse
1848	New Jersey Telegraph Company	Philadelphia and New York	Downing	New Jersey	$100,000	House

(continued)

Table 8.3 (continued)

Date	*Name*	*Location*	*Original promoter*	*State of Incorp.*	*Original capital*	*Patent*
4/20/49	Boston and New York Telegraph Company	Boston and New York	Downing	Mass	$120,000	House
11/10/48	Western Telegraph Company	Baltimore, Wheeling, and Pittsburgh	Morse	Maryland		Morse
1848–1849	Erie and Michigan Telegraph Company	Buffalo and Milwaukee	Smith	New York	$203,000	Morse
1/49	People's Telegraph Company	Cincinnati and New Orleans	O'Rielly			Barnes & Zook/Bain
1/49	Maine Telegraph Company	Portland and Calais	Alden	Maine		Morse
1849	Ohio, Indiana, and Illinois Telegraph Company	Dayton, Toledo, Indianapolis, and Chicago	O'Rielly	Illinois	$240,050	Morse
1849	North American Telegraph Company	Washington and New York		Pennsylvania	$125,000	Bain
4/11/49	Illinois and Mississippi Telegraph Company	St. Louis, Chicago, Iowa, and Indiana	O'Rielly	Illinois	$500,000	Morse/Pirate/Bain
4/19/49	New York and New England Telegraph Company	Boston and New York	O'Rielly		$42,300	Bain
1850	New York State Telegraph Company	New York and Buffalo	O'Rielly	New York	Unknown	Bain
1850	New York State Printing Telegraph Company	New York and Buffalo	Selden	New York	$200,000	House

Date	*Name*	*Location*	*Original promoter*	*State of Incorp.*	*Original capital*	*Patent*
1/51	New Orleans and Ohio Telegraph Company	New Orleans and Pittsburgh	Morse	Kentucky, Tenn., Miss		Morse
4/1/51	N.Y. and Mississippi Valley Telegraph Company	Buffalo and St. Louis	Selden	New York	$360,000	House
10/1/55	American Telegraph Company	East Coast		New York switched to N.J. in 1859	$200,000 $740,000	
1/60	Southwestern Telegraph Company	Pittsburgh and New Orleans	Green	Kentucky, Tenn., Miss. and Louisiana	$600,000	
8/3/64	United States Telegraph Company	National		New York	$6 million	

Source Law, Emerging Technology, and Market Structure: The Development of the Telegraph Industry, 1838–1868. Table 2.1. Tomas W. Nonnenmacher, *PhD. Dissertation*. 1995

has the lowest spreads. Did the NYSE emerge as the winner of this competition because it was more efficient than the other two exchanges?

Market Efficiency
To test the hypothesis that the most efficient exchange was the winner; bid ask spreads are analyzed. Average spreads for each exchange are compared. In addition, spreads for the same day across New York and Philadelphia are compared for Reading Railroad, a cross-listed security.

(A) Average spreads: Data for the last recorded day of each month are taken as a proxy for the month. For a security for which both the bid and the ask price are reported, average bid ask spreads are calculated as follows: for an individual security the difference between bid and ask price is taken. This constitutes the numerator. The average of the bid and ask price is the denominator. The result of this fraction is recorded for an individual security. The results for all the securities for that day are then averaged to get the average spread on a particular day, for an exchange. The average bid ask spread thus computed for each of the three exchanges is reported in Graph 8.3. For each month of a particular year, the year itself is recorded. There are three series, corresponding to each of the three exchanges. Data for Graph 8.3 are in Appendix B.

Graph 8.3 shows us that the NYSE had lower average spreads from 1837 to 1841, and again in 1843. For period 1846–1852, which was

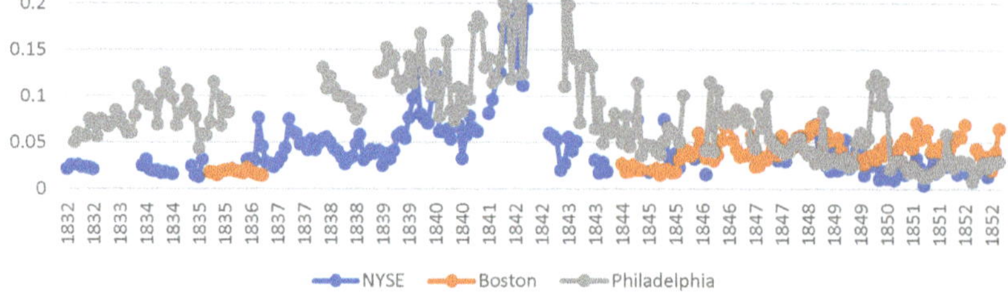

Graph. 8.3 Average bid ask spreads 1832–1852

one of intense competition among the three exchanges, there was no clear winner in terms of average spreads.

Investors could use the telegraph to trade shares, even before the telegraph became a reliable means of communication. This could be done by paying for both sending the message to its destination and paying to have it transmitted back again to check if the message had been accurately transmitted. This increased reliability came at an increase in both the time taken and the monetary cost of sending a message. Hence, though the telegraph was being used to trade shares in 1850–1851, its use pre 1852 would have been much less, as compared to its use post 1852.

In 1851–1852, average spreads for each of the exchanges decreased, and these spreads moved closer to each other. This supports the idea that the telegraph led to increased competition among the exchanges.

(B) Individual spreads: Spreads on the NYSE and on the Philadelphia exchange for Reading Railroad shares are compared for the same day on each exchange. Philadelphia and New York were linked by the telegraph in 1846. Prior to the advent of the telegraph, arbitrage opportunities existed between the different exchanges. Individuals were always looking for ways to take advantage of these arbitrage opportunities. Two methods one using flags and the other using mirrors were used to transmit stock market information between Philadelphia and New York prior to the advent of the telegraph. The telegraph was a definite improvement over these two methods, and individuals would have begun to use it as soon as it was available; even before it became a reliable means of communication.

In case we want to study differences in bid ask spreads between the two exchanges for the shares of Reading Railroad to discover if the NYSE had lower spreads, we should do this for the period before the advent of the telegraph. Once the telegraph was available to arbitrage away the differences, differences in spreads, at least in recorded data would be rarer to find, as they would have been traded away by arbitrageurs. As mentioned above, even before the telegraph, there were individuals arbitraging on securities that were traded on more than one exchange. The telegraph, even in its earlier years, was a vast improvement over the other methods in use at the time. Thus; we may not observe any instances of differences in bid ask spreads after the advent of the telegraph.

Data on bid ask spreads for Reading Railroad from July 1846 to December 1846 and for two days in September 1852 are presented in Table 8.4. During this period, both exchanges reported data for Mondays.

The methodology used for calculating these spreads is as follows: for the NYSE, the simple bid ask spread is computed, i.e., the ask price–the bid price. As the par value of the security on the Philadelphia Stock Exchange is half of the par value of the security on the NYSE, the spread on the Philadelphia Stock Exchange is doubled for purposes of comparison.

The par value of the security traded was $100 on the New York Stock Exchange (NYSE) and $50 on the Philadelphia Stock Exchange (PSE)

For the NYSE, the bid and ask price are recorded as reported. The spread is then calculated by subtracting the bid price from the ask price

For the PSE, the bid and ask price are recorded as reported. The bid and the ask price are then doubled to make the numbers comparable to those on the NYSE. The spread is then calculated by subtracting the bid price from the ask price

Key: ? = The fraction following the price was undecipherable

Source Contemporary Newspapers as detailed in Table 6.1

The results are as follows. The NYSE generally had the lower spread. December 28 is the only exception. On this day, both the NYSE and the Philadelphia Stock Exchange had the same spread. The difference in the spreads varied from 25 cents per share to over six dollars a share. It was more common for the difference in the spread to be 25 cents or 50 cents.

Table 8.4 reveals that in the year of the installation of telegraph lines; there were differences in the spread on the two exchanges and that when this occurred, the NYSE had the lower spread. Once the telegraph became a reliable means of communication, for reasons mentioned above, it is reasonable to expect that at least in recorded data, differences in spreads would be rarer to find.

The NYSE had lower spreads prior to the commercial use of the telegraph. The bid ask spread is a cost of doing business and a measure of efficiency. Thus, we note that the exchange with the lower costs, i.e., the more efficient exchange prior to competition eventually became the pre-eminent exchange.

As the NYSE was typically larger than the other two exchanges for the period under consideration,[6] it is reasonable to assume that two other costs of trading shares; (i) the time taken to find a matching trade and

[6] On 31st May 1848, the value of securities traded on the Boston Stock Exchange was greater than the value of securities traded on the NYSE, and on the Philadelphia Exchange.

Table 8.4 Bid ask spreads for Reading Railroad

	NYC			*PSE*		
July 6, 1846, Monday	Bid	Asked	Spread	Bid	Asked	Spread
				38.125	34.75	
	68.0	68.5	0.5	76.25	68.75	
July 13, 1846, Monday	Bid	Asked	Spread	Bid	Asked	Spread
				33		
	66	67	1	66		
July 20, 1846, Monday	Bid	Asked	Spread	Bid	Asked	Spread
				34.25	34.5	
	68.75	69	0.25	68.5	69	0.5
Aug 3, 1846, Monday	Bid	Asked	Spread	Bid	Asked	Spread
				30.875	34	
	67.5	67.5	0	61.75	68	6.25
Aug 24, 1846, Monday	Bid	Asked	Spread	Bid	Asked	Spread
				33.375		
	67			66.75		
Sep 14, 1846, Monday	Bid	Asked	Spread	Bid	Asked	Spread
				31.75	32.125	
	63.25	63.25	0	63.5	64.25	0.75
Sep. 21, 1846, Monday	Bid	Asked	Spread	Bid	Asked	Spread
				32	32.25	
	64			64	64.5	0.5
Sep 28, 1846, Monday	Bid	Asked	Spread	Bid	Asked	Spread
				32?	32?	
	65	65.25	0.25	?	?	

(continued)

Table 8.4 (continued)

	NYC			*PSE*		
Oct 5, 1846, Monday	Bid	Asked	Spread	Bid	Asked	Spread
				32	32?	
	65.25	65.75	0.5	64	?	
Oct 12, 1846, Monday	Bid	Asked	Spread	Bid	Asked	Spread
				32?	32?	
				?	?	
				32	32.125	
				64	64.25	0.25
	64.5	64.75	0.25			
	63	63.5	0.5			
Nov 2, 1846, Monday	Bid	Asked	Spread	Bid	Asked	Spread
				31.125	32	
				62.25	64	1.75
				31.75	32	
				63.5	64	0.5
	63	63.25	0.25			
	63	63.25	0.25			
Nov 16, 1846, Monday	Bid	Asked	Spread	Bid	Asked	Spread
				31?	31?	
	62.5	62.875	0.375	?	?	
Nov 23, 1846, Monday	Bid	Asked	Spread	Bid	Asked	Spread
				31.375	31.5	
		63		62.75	62.5	

	NYC			*PSE*		
Nov 23, 1846, Monday	Bid	Asked	Spread	Bid	Asked	Spread
				31.5	31.625	
				63	63.25	0.25
				31.125	31.625	
				62.25	63.25	1
	63	63	0			
	63	63	0			
Dec 7, 1846, Monday	Bid	Asked	Spread	Bid	Asked	Spread
				31	31?/8	
	62.625	62.625	0	62		
Dec 14, 1846, Monday	Bid	Asked	Spread	Bid	Asked	Spread
				31.75	31?	
	62.75	62.75	0	63.5		
Dec 21, 1846, Monday	Bid	Asked	Spread	Bid	Asked	Spread
				31	31.125	
	61.5			62	62.25	0.25
Dec 28, 1846, Monday	Bid	Asked	Spread	Bid	Asked	Spread
				31	31.125	
	61.25	61.5	0.25	62	62.25	0.25

(continued)

Table 8.4 (continued)

	NYC			*PSE*		
Sep 13, 1852	Bid	Asked	Spread	Bid	Asked	Spread
				47.125	47.25	
				94.25	94.5	0.25
Sep 14, 1852	Bid	Asked	Spread	Bid	Asked	Spread
	94.25	94.5	0.25			

(ii) the price movement against the entity initiating the trade would also both be lower on the NYSE.

The NYSE was the most efficient exchange prior to competition and it eventually became the national exchange, with Boston and Philadelphia remaining regional exchanges. This is just part of the story. We need to look at the event that caused the exchanges to come into competition with each other, i.e., the adoption of the telegraph in more detail.

Use of the Telegraph for Trading Securities at Geographically Distant Locations

The book "Historical Sketch of the Electric Telegraph: Including its Rise and Progress in the United States." by Jones, Alexander. *George P. Putnam, 10 Park Place, New York. 1852.* contains the details of a survey that was conducted for 1850–51 and the book was published in 1852. This survey was conducted among the managers of four major telegraph lines. These were

1. The O'Reilly Line
2. The Bain Line
3. The House's Line
4. Morse's New-York and Buffalo Line

Questions were asked relating, *inter alia*, to the reliability of the telegraph; the longest distance over which messages were sent; the revenue of various lines; and the different purposes for which the telegraph was used.

The survey had 16 questions. Questions 10, 13, and 14 are of relevance to this discussion. These questions and the relevant answers are reproduced here. The answers are the ones provided by O' Reilly at his Telegraph Line Office, 180 Broadway.

> "Question 10. To what extent is the telegraph used for commercial correspondence? This would be best illustrated by the expenses incurred by two or three of the greatest commercial houses.
>
> Answers: It is used to a great extent, in conveying secrets of rise and fall of markets; ... There are brokers, bankers, &c., in Wall-street, that receive and send, on an average, six to ten messages per day, throughout the year.

13. Are interruptions frequent, arising from atmospheric electricity?

Answers: Interruptions from atmospheric electricity have been greatly reduced of late, and it is confidently expected that they will, at no distant day, be entirely overcome.

14. Or from other, and what causes? (Answered as part of Question 13.) Other causes of interruption are accidental, trees, &c., falling on the wire and snapping it."[7]

This survey reveals that by 1850–1851, the telegraph was being used to trade shares, especially for arbitrage purposes when the markets were very volatile. It also reveals that there remained some problems with the reliability of the telegraph in 1850–1851. This survey along with Tomas Nonnenmacher's dissertation establishes the following:

a. By 1850–1851, the telegraph was being used to send buy and sell orders for securities being traded at geographically distant markets though there were issues with the reliability of the telegraph.
b. The telegraph was widespread by 1852, and major cities in north-eastern US were linked by the telegraph
c. It was only by 1852 that the telegraph became a reliable means of communication.

Graphs 7.1, 7.2, and 7.3 show the NYSE began its rise to pre-eminence in 1851–1852; and that this process accelerated after 1852. Thus, we are led to believe that the telegraph is the reason for the rise of the NYSE to pre-eminence.

The telegraph provided for almost instantaneous communication between geographically distant points. Prior to the commercial use of the telegraph, arbitrage opportunities existed between New York and Philadelphia. The telegraph reduced the cost of communication between cities. It is natural to expect that once the telegraph became a reliable means of communication, some, or all these arbitrage opportunities would be traded away.

[7] Jones, Alexander "Historical Sketch of the Electric Telegraph: Including Its Rise and Progress in the United States." George P. Putnam, 10 Park Place, New York. 1852.

The telegraph became a reliable means of communication by 1852. However, even in 1850–1851, it was a much better method of communication as compared to the alternatives.

One of the issues with reliability when transmitting messages was the level of accuracy with which messages were transmitted. This improved gradually as telegraph operators gained experience.

For people willing to pay for it, there was a way to improve the accuracy of a message. The person wishing to transmit a message, paid for transmitting the message and paid to have the message transmitted back to check for accuracy. Hence, even before 1852, the telegraph could be used to transmit messages more accurately than the alternatives it replaced.

Trading in Cross-Listed Securities

A security is called a cross-listed security if it is listed on more than one exchange. Reading Railroad was a security that was listed and traded on both the NYSE and the Philadelphia Stock Exchange.

The NYSE had the lower spreads before the telegraph became a reliable means of communication. Once the telegraph became a viable means of communication, one would expect some orders for securities that were traded on both the NYSE and on the Philadelphia Exchange to flow from the Philadelphia Stock Exchange to the NYSE.

Data on the value of trade in Reading Railroad stock at the NYSE and at the Philadelphia Stock Exchange (PSE) are presented in Table 8.5.

Graph 8.4 shows the value of trade in Reading Railroad stock at the NYSE and at the Philadelphia Stock Exchange (PSE).

Graph 8.5 shows the number of trades for Reading Railroad at the NYSE and at the Philadelphia Stock Exchange (PSE). As the par value of the Reading Railroad stock was \$100 on the NYSE, and \$50 on the PSE, the number of trades on the PSE has been adjusted (divided by two), to make the numbers comparable.

Table 8.5 Reading Railroad value of shares traded USD ($). 1846–1855

		NYSE	*PSE*
Jan	1846	8850	20,300
Feb	1846	34,650	10,275
Mar	1846	7275	
Apr	1846	38,163	3475
May	1846	25,600	
Jun	1846	30,850	1700
Jul	1846	37,269	11,638
Aug	1846	49,213	
Sep	1846	29,084	
Oct	1846	23,794	
Nov	1846	7570	
Dec	1846	4663	1538
Jan	1847	21,916	6993
Feb	1847	82,114	7250
Mar	1847	14,731	1450
Apr	1847	35,738	15,394
May	1847	49,331	4313
Jun	1847		46,725
Jul	1847	36,625	3325
Aug	1847	16,588	3004
Sep	1847	12,750	3188
Oct	1847	97,931	13,500
Nov	1847	84,131	1513
Dec	1847	54,575	18,938
Jan	1848	65,194	2400
Feb	1848	8513	3181
Mar	1848		2744
Apr	1848	11,575	
May	1848	28,275	
Jun	1848		
Jul	1848		
Aug	1848	6400	1280
Sep	1848	14,188	1569
Oct	1848		
Nov	1848	9924	2850
Dec	1848	40,725	356
Jan	1849	25,438	638
Feb	1849	20,338	7738
Mar	1849	8250	4125
Apr	1849	9600	
May	1849		7349
Jun	1849	12,163	10,250

(continued)

Table 8.5 (continued)

		NYSE	*PSE*
Jul	1849	126,925	
Aug	1849	10,188	5950
Sep	1849	4981	2400
Oct	1849		
Nov	1849	127,638	6169
Dec	1849	83,700	5600
Jan	1850	52,875	18,331
Feb	1850		23,700
Mar	1850	14,300	
Apr	1850	16,500	23,794
May	1850	57,956	46,975
Jun	1850	50,163	9863
Jul	1850		12,069
Aug	1850	84,281	32,088
Sep	1850	122,945	50,950
Oct	1850	99,750	19,975
Nov	1850	292,186	77,844
Dec	1850	149,746	69,906
Jan	1851	195,400	160,256
Feb	1851	45,750	16,863
Mar	1851	105,833	46,070
Apr	1851	116,763	37,225
May	1851	335,945	77,088
Jun	1851	61,111	49,175
Jul	1851	204,850	34,057
Aug	1851	163,006	40,183
Sep	1851	60,775	39,406
Oct	1851	92,144	18,865
Nov	1851	153,700	60,900
Dec	1851	115,250	16,106
Jan	1852	212,675	52,688
Feb	1852	415,900	133,906
Mar	1852	170,369	55,931
Apr	1852	230,338	39,050
May	1852	42,913	7850
Jun	1852	182,556	57,813
Jul	1852	116,088	4463
Aug	1852	18,800	14,100
Sep	1852	9825	
Oct	1852	24,363	
Nov	1852		
Dec	1852	9800	4900

(continued)

Table 8.5 (continued)

		NYSE	*PSE*
Jan	1853	12,800	
Feb	1853	13,388	
Mar	1853	10,680	
Apr	1853	30,287	31,650
May	1853	13,288	2219
Jun	1853	51,188	
Jul	1853	44,000	
Aug	1853	42,200	5628
Sep	1853	58,575	12,600
Oct	1853	26,000	3644
Nov	1853	103,000	
Dec	1853	43,085	23,825
Jan	1854	75,675	23,648
Feb	1854	114,993	13,169
Mar	1854	272,108	7108
Apr	1854	22,538	38,274
May	1854	176,469	32,460
Jun	1854	241,763	11,675
Jul	1854	87,644	25,994
Aug	1854	88,938	30,975
Sep	1854	342,140	17,069
Oct	1854	139,083	9469
Nov	1854	217,759	15,464
Dec	1854	236,400	11,813
Jan	1855	93,288	
Feb	1855	174,275	9606
Mar	1855	170,203	6656
Apr	1855	546,544	24,875
May	1855	607,875	26,425
Jun	1855	172,919	23,872
Jul	1855	443,575	7709
Aug	1855	634,419	72,414
Sep	1855	591,537	75,748
Oct	1855	471,725	43,645
Nov	1855	315,461	13,924
Dec	1855	404,375	14,262

Source Contemporary Newspapers as detailed in Table 6.1

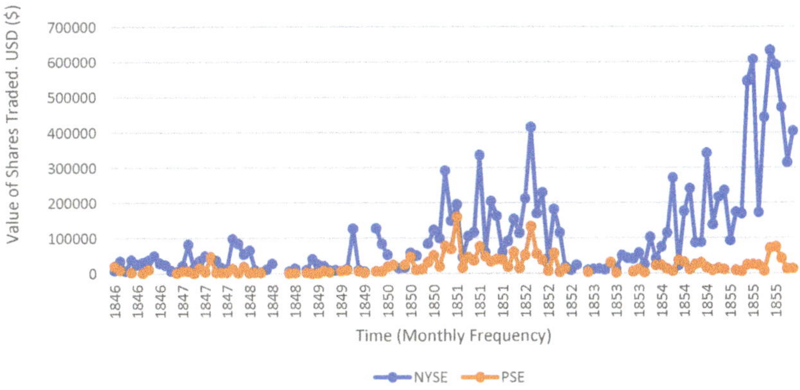

Graph 8.4 Reading Railroad. Value of shares traded. Monthly. 1846–1855

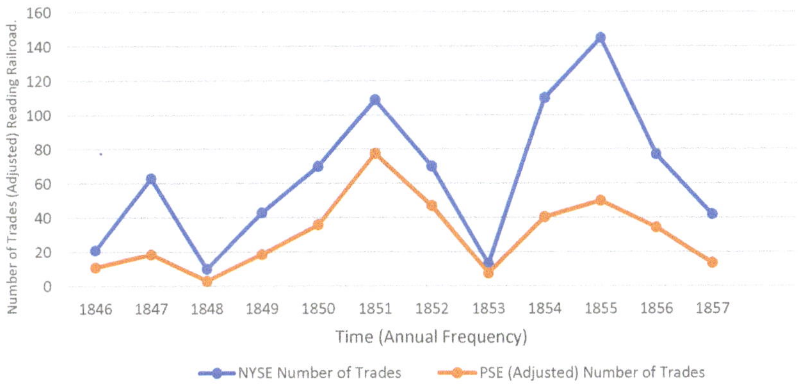

Graph 8.5 Number of trades (adjusted for PSE) Reading Railroad. Annual. 1846–1857

For Graphs 8.6a–f, the following have been defined:

"Large Size" Trades of Size 500+ shares.
"Medium Size" Trades of Size 100–500 shares.
"Small Size" Trades of Size 1–100 shares.

For the Philadelphia Stock Exchange (PSE in the graphs), the numbers have been adjusted to account for the fact that par value on NYSE is $100, and $50 on the Philadelphia Stock Exchange (PSE).

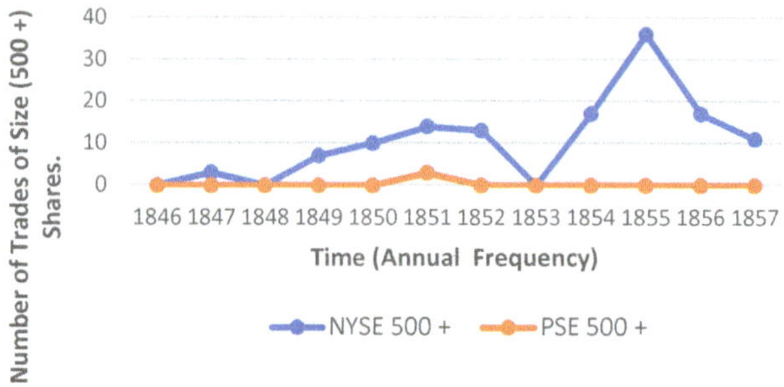

Graph 8.6a Large trades. Number of trades of size (500+) shares. 1846–1857

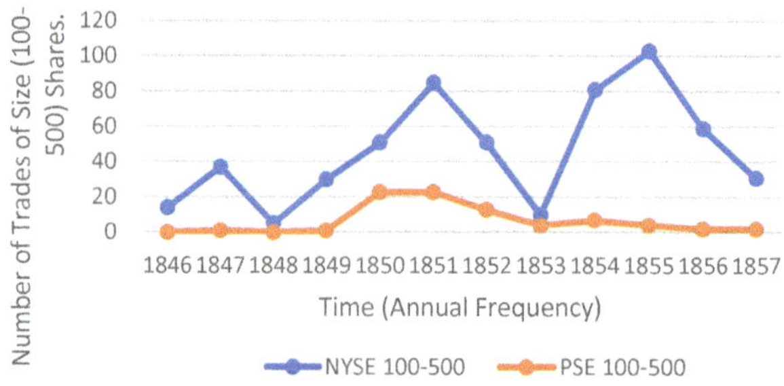

Graph 8.6b Medium trades. Number of trades of size (100–500) shares. 1846–1857

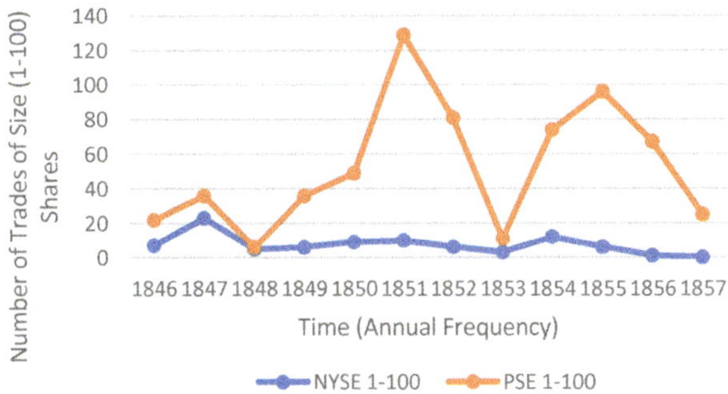

Graph 8.6c Small trades. Number of trades of size (1–100) shares. 1846–1857

Graphs 8.6d, 8.6e, 8.6f look at the relative proportions of these on the NYSE and PSE.

Graph 8.6d shows the proportion of Large Trades on the NYSE and the PSE.

$$\text{Proportion of Large Trades on the NYSE} = \frac{\text{Number of Large Trades on the NYSE}}{(\text{Total Number of Large Trades on NYSE} + \text{PSE})}$$

$$\text{Proportion of Large Trades on the PSE} = \frac{\text{Number of Large Trades on PSE}}{(\text{Total Number of Large Trades on NYSE} + \text{PSE})}$$

Graph 8.6e shows the proportion of Medium Trades on the NYSE and the PSE.

$$\text{Proportion of Medium Trades on the NYSE} = \frac{\text{Number of Medium Trades on the NYSE}}{(\text{Total Number of Medium Trades on NYSE} + \text{PSE})}$$

$$\text{Proportion of Medium Trades on the PSE} = \frac{\text{Number of Medium Trades on the PSE}}{(\text{Total Number of Medium Trades on NYSE} + \text{PSE})}$$

Graph 8.6f shows the proportion of Small Trades on the NYSE and the PSE.

$$\text{Proportion of Small Trades on NYSE} = \frac{\text{Number of Small Trades on the NYSE}}{(\text{Total Number of Small Trades on NYSE} + \text{PSE})}$$

$$\text{Proportion of Small Trades on the PSE} = \frac{\text{Number of Small Trades on the PSE}}{(\text{Total Number of Small Trades on NYSE} + \text{PSE})}$$

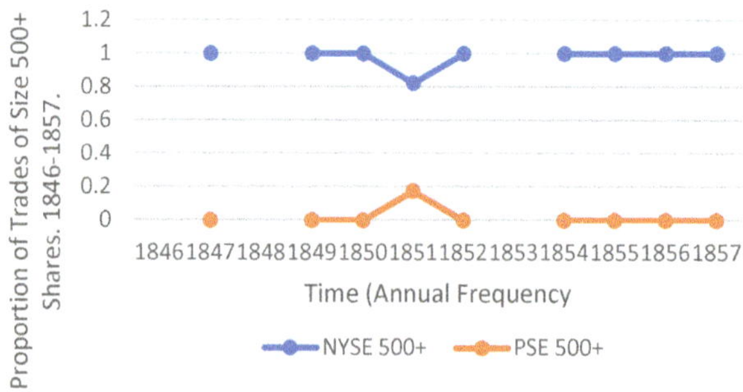

Graph 8.6d Proportion of large trades. (Trades of size 500+ shares). 1846–1857

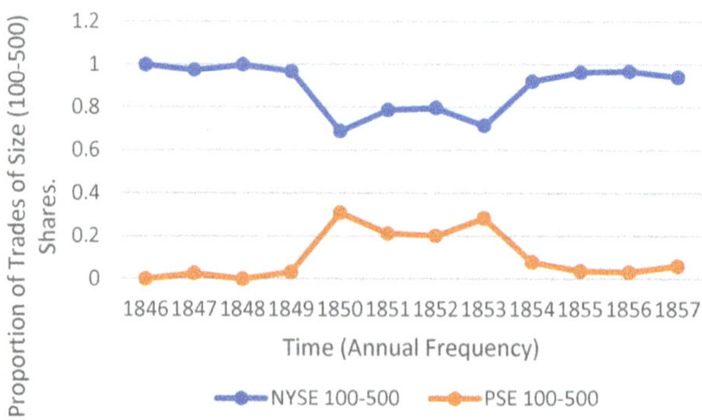

Graph 8.6e Proportion of medium trades. (Trades of size [100–500] shares). 1846–1857

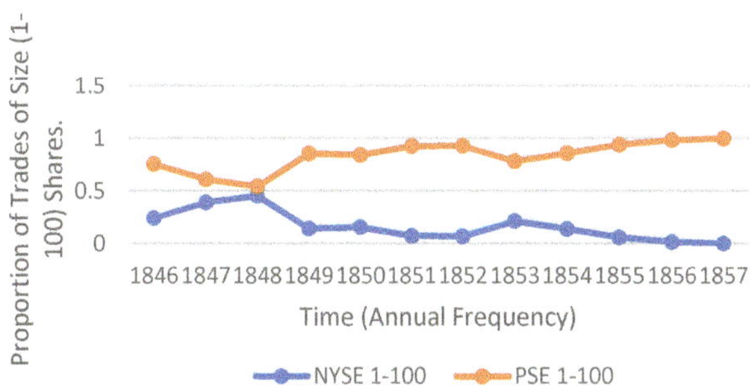

Graph 8.6f Proportion of small trades. (Trades of size [1–100] shares). 1846–1857

Graphs 8.6a–f are based on the data in Table 8.6.

Graphs 8.6d shows the proportion of Large Trades on the NYSE and the PSE

Graphs 8.6e shows the proportion of Medium Trades on the NYSE and the PSE

Table 8.6 Reading railroad size of trades

Year	*NYSE 1–100*	*PSE 1–100*	*NYSE 100–500*	*PSE 100–500*	*NYSE 500+*	*PSE 500+*
1846	7	22	14	0	0	0
1847	23	36	37	1	3	0
1848	5	6	5	0	0	0
1849	6	36	30	1	7	0
1850	9	49	51	23	10	0
1851	10	129	85	23	14	3
1852	6	81	51	13	13	0
1853	3	11	10	4	0	0
1854	12	74	81	7	17	0
1855	6	96	103	4	36	0
1856	1	67	59	2	17	0
1857	0	25	31	2	11	0

New York Stock Exchange (NYSE). Philadelphia Stock Exchange (PSE)

For Reading Railroad shares: par value on the NYSE $100 and the PSE $ 50; number of trades of each size, on the PSE adjusted for this

Graphs 8.6a–f analyze the large, medium, and small trading lots on the NYSE and the PSE

Graphs 8.6a–c look at the number of times that a large size, medium size, and small size trade occurred on these exchanges

Graphs 8.6f shows the proportion of Small Trades on the NYSE and the PSE

Graphs 8.6a–c show the number of trades of different sizes for Reading Railroad on the NYSE and the Philadelphia Stock Exchange (PSE). Graphs 8.6d–f show the proportion of trades of different sizes for Reading Railroad on the NYSE and the PSE.

Graphs 8.6a and 8.6d reveal that for the period under consideration, "Large" Trades were chiefly conducted on the NYSE. Only in 1851, when the telegraph brought the two exchanges into competition with each other, were there three "Large" Trade executed on the Philadelphia Stock Exchange. This did not occur again during the period under consideration.

If the trading volume on the Philadelphia Stock Exchange was large enough in 1851 for investors to execute a "Large" Trade there, the trading volume should have been adequate post 1851 too. The fact that there were no more "Large" Trades executed on the Philadelphia Stock Exchange post 1851, means that either (i) that no one for whom the Philadelphia Stock Exchange was the nearest exchange, wished to execute "Large" Trades or (ii) that people for whom the Philadelphia Stock Exchange was the nearest exchange, given that they could now trade on the NYSE, preferred to trade on the NYSE.

From this information, we can infer that for a brief period, investors felt comfortable executing "Large" Size trades on the Philadelphia Stock Exchange, and that once the telegraph became a reliable means of communication, investors once again chose to execute "Large" Trades only on the NYSE.

A "Large Order" (500+ shares on the NYSE and 1000+ shares on the Philadelphia Stock Exchange) was a substantial part of the average daily volume. In 1851, the daily average number of shares traded on the NYSE for Reading Railroad was 2420.83 shares. 500 shares were 20.65% of this. The daily average number of shares traded on the Philadelphia Stock Exchange for Reading Railroad in 1851 was 1722.92 shares. 1000 shares was 58.04% of this.

A single transaction of even 20% of the daily trading volume is a very large transaction size. This is even more so for a single transaction that is 58% of the market. It is not surprising therefore that there were no "Large Orders" for Reading Railroad either before or after 1851. One can only postulate that by 1851 the increased use of the telegraph to send buy and sell orders increased trading volume of Reading Railroad shares on the Philadelphia Stock Exchange to a level that people felt comfortable executing "Large" Orders there.

Three possible scenarios can explain why "Large Lots" were traded on the PSE only in 1851. There is no data at present to support any of these arguments. Prior to 1851, people in Philadelphia holding Reading Railroad shares of par value of $50, and wishing to trade in "Large Lots" broke up the order into "Medium Lots" or "Small Lots" and traded these on the PSE. Or people in Philadelphia held shares of par value of $100 and executed the orders on the NYSE. Another less likely explanation is that no one for whom the Philadelphia Stock Exchange was the nearest exchange, wished to trade in "Large Lots" prior to 1851.

Regarding the lack of any "Large Lots" trade on the PSE post 1851, one can only postulate that given the lower costs of trading shares on the NYSE; it was worthwhile for traders of "Large Lots" of shares who earlier traded on the Philadelphia Stock Exchange to now hold shares of par value of $100 and to send their orders to be executed on the floor of the NYSE.

Graphs 8.6b shows that "Medium Size" lots were traded on the PSE in 1847, 1849 (1 instance each); 1850, 1851 (23 instances each); 1852 (13 instances); 1853 (4 instances); 1854 (7 instances); 1855 (4 instances) and; 1856, 1857 (2 instances each). There was an increase in the instances in 1850 and 1851. 1852 had 13 instances, which compared to the numbers before 1850 and after 1852 is a large number. Graphs 8.6e, shows an increase in proportion of "Medium Lots" on the Philadelphia Stock Exchange in 1850, and 1851; and to a smaller extent in 1852. Though the number of medium trades on the PSE reduced to 4 in 1853, the proportion of trades on the PSE increased, as the number of "Medium Lot" trades on the NYSE in 1853 fell to 10 (as compared to 51 in 1850; 85 in 1851; and 51in 1852). Post 1853 the proportion of "Medium Lots" trades on the PSE declined to pre-1850 levels

From 1852 onwards, it became easier and cheaper for people for whom the PSE was the nearest exchange, to trade on the NYSE. People interested in holding and trading in "Large Lots" and "Medium Lots" would have preferred to trade on the NYSE. To do so, they could hold shares of a par value of $100 instead of $50.

Arguments put forward for the trading in "Large Lots" on the PSE, extends, to a smaller extent to the trading in "Medium Lots." It is interesting to note that the relative uptick in trading in "Medium Lots" started before that for "Large Lots," and continued for a year longer. The only explanation, once again, not supported by data at present, is that much more volume was required for an investor to feel comfortable trading in "Large Lots" as compared to the volume required for trading in "Medium Lots."

By 1852, a ten-word telegram sent from New York City to Philadelphia cost 25 cents for the first 10 words, and 2 cents for each additional word.[8] Given this cost of sending or receiving information, and transmitting orders via the telegraph and other costs related with conducting business at a geographically distant location, it may not have been financially viable for investors wishing to trade "Small Lots" to trade at a geographically distant location. Given the cost of sending a telegraphic message in the 1850s, traders in Philadelphia of "Small Lots" trades would have found it more beneficial to continue trading on the PSE.

Conclusion

A stock exchange has economies of scale. Innovations in transport and communication technology that lead to the expansion of the geographical scope of the market initiate changes in the industrial organization of securities markets, leading first to increased competition and eventually to a single exchange emerging as the primary exchange for cross-listed securities.

The analysis in previous sections has already revealed that the NYSE had the lowest spreads among the three exchanges under consideration. The telegraph allowed investors to choose among exchanges. We note that aggregate trading on the NYSE increased after 1851–1852 and this process accelerated after 1852.

Prior to the advent of the telegraph, the NYSE was more efficient than either Boston or Philadelphia, providing a lower cost for trading securities. The telegraph by allowing investors a choice among exchanges helped begin the rise of the NYSE to pre-eminence. Innovations in communications technology over the next few decades continued and accelerated this trend.

[8] Jones, Alexander "Historical Sketch of the Electric Telegraph: Including Its Rise and Progress in the United States." George P. Putnam, 10 Park Place, New York. 1852.

I reach the following conclusions:

a. The NYSE began its rise to pre-eminence in 1851–1852. This process accelerated post 1852.
b. This began a process of transformation of the structure of securities markets. A market structure with several local or regional exchanges was transformed into one where there was one national exchange and several regional exchanges.
c. The telegraph is the most probable reason for this transformation.

Growth of Existing Exchanges and Emergence of New Exchanges After 1852

The 1800s saw rapid changes in transport and communications. Among these changes, the telegraph, by providing almost instantaneous communication between geographically distant exchanges, gave the first boost to the NYSE, by causing trade in cross-listed securities to move to the NYSE. Prior to the advent of the telegraph, the NYSE was larger and more efficient than the other two exchanges. However, investors that were geographically distant from the NYSE could not take advantage of this. Thus, Philadelphia and Boston were also important places to trade cross-listed securities, with trading on each exchange being determined by the interest of investors in close geographical proximity to an exchange. There was some arbitrage among exchanges using predecessors to the telegraph, however this type of arbitrage was very risky, and differences in bid ask spreads continued to persist.

The telegraph, by allowing investors the choice among several exchanges, started the rise of the NYSE to pre-eminence. The introduction of the telegraph by no means completed the process of the NYSE's rise to pre-eminence. Subsequent innovations in transport and communications over the next few decades continued this process.

At the same time, newer exchanges emerged both within New York City and in cities outside the north-eastern US.

Within New York City itself, several exchanges survived and did well. For most of the time, these complemented the NYSE rather than competed with it. The Curb Exchange that later became the American Stock Exchange, traded newer, less established securities that did not interest the NYSE. As these securities became more reliable, and the companies they represented became large enough, they moved to the NYSE, with the Curb Exchange taking on other, newer, less established securities. Other exchanges that competed with the NYSE were either eventually absorbed by it, or competed out of existence.

A question that comes to mind when one reads this book is the following: If, (i) a stock exchange has economies of scale; (ii) the NYSE was the most efficient exchange when the telegraph began to be used for trading securities at exchanges outside a potential investor's city or state stock exchanges, and (iii) the NYSE gained business at the expense of other exchanges after 1852, then how do we explain the emergence of new exchanges after 1852?

The explanation is as follows: There were monetary and other costs associated with sending and receiving messages via the telegraph.

The monetary cost of sending a telegraph depended on (i) the physical distance over which the messages were transmitted and (ii) the level of competition for transmitting the message.

The accuracy with which a message was transmitted depended upon (i) the physical distance over which the message was transmitted (ii) the number of times it had to be re-transmitted before it reached its final destination and (iii) the number of different telegraph companies that were involved in the re-transmission (if the message was re-transmitted).

Ceteris paribus, places that were farther apart, had to pay higher prices for sending and receiving messages than places that were closer to each other. The accuracy with which messages were transmitted was, *ceteris paribus*, inversely related to the distance over which the message had to be transmitted.

Table 8.7 in Appendix C has data on the cost of sending telegraphic messages from New York City to other cities in the United States and Canada. An abstract is presented here as Table 8.7 (Abstract). The highest costs were for New Orleans: 240 cents for the first ten words and 14 cents for each additional word. The lowest costs; for several cities: were 20 cents for the first ten words and 1 cent for each additional word.

Thus, as new regions developed, they had their own exchanges. Eventually, though, as costs of communications fell, these exchanges increasingly became places to find the best execution in trading of securities not traded on the NYSE. They either remained regional exchanges or became the primary place to trade instruments that were different in nature to those being traded on the NYSE, such as options and futures.

Table 8.7 (Abstract): Charges for Telegraph dispatches from New York City as reported in 1852

(Abstract): Cost for transmission in cents (1/100 USD)			
City	*State/country*	*Ten words*	*Each additional word*
Baton Rouge	La.	235	16
Boston	Mass.	20	2
Carmel	N.Y.	20	1
Catskill	N.Y.	20	1
Chicago	Ill.	100	6
Cold Spring	N.Y.	20	1
Coxsackie	N.Y.	20	1
Kingston	N.Y.	20	1
Newburg	N.Y.	20	1
New Orleans	La.	240	14
Peekskill	N.Y.	20	1
Philadelphia	Pa.	25	2
Piermont	N.Y.	20	1
Poughkeepsie	N.Y.	20	1
Reading	Pa.	40	4
Red Hook	N.Y.	20	1
Rondout	N.Y.	20	1
Valatia	N.Y.	20	1

Source Jones, Alexander "Historical Sketch of the Electric Telegraph: Including its Rise and Progress in the United States." George P. Putnam, 10 Park Place, New York. 1852. Listed in the Table of Contents as: Chapter XIX. Charges for Dispatches from New York to all parts of the United States and Canada. Cost of Transmitting Telegraphic Messages. Page 187 onwards. Appears as Chapter XX: Charges for Telegraph Dispatches, Pages 189 to 194

Some new exchanges emerged after 1852, in New York City itself. One of these, the Curb Exchange complemented the NYSE. Others were either absorbed by the NYSE or eliminated due to competition.

A paper titled: "Competing with the New York Stock Exchange" William O. Brown, Jr; J. Harold Mulherin; and Marc D. Weidenmier (*The Quarterly Journal of Economics*, Nov., 2008, Vol. 123, No. 4 [Nov., 2008], pp. 1679–1719), discusses the Consolidated Stock Exchange of New York. The paper states that: "We examine the largely forgotten but unparalleled episode of competition between the NYSE and the Consolidated Stock Exchange of New York (Consolidated) from 1885 to 1926. The Consolidated averaged 23% of NYSE volume for approximately forty years by operating a second market for the most liquid securities that traded on the Big Board. Our results suggest that NYSE bid ask spreads fell by more than 10% when the Consolidated began to trade NYSE stocks and subsequently increased when the Consolidated ceased operations. The empirical analysis suggests that this historical episode of stock market competition improved consumer welfare by an amount equivalent to US$9.6 billion.[9]" They further state that "Using its location to gain access to the latest information on Wall Street, the Consolidated attracted trading in NYSE listings by charging lower commissions, offering odd-lot trading, and allowing a longer settlement period.[10]"

In a market where firms have positive network externalities, which *inter alia* lead to economies of scale, one way for a new entrant to compete with the existing natural monopolist, which by dint of its size will have lower bid ask spreads, is to offer even lower spreads.

New exchanges will continue to emerge. The fact that stock exchanges face falling average costs leads us to expect the following. Given the constraints of communications technology, there shall be a single venue where buyers and sellers of a particular security will naturally converge.

Stock markets have positive network externalities, which *inter alia* lead to economies of scale. So do firms in other markets for services such as (i) Taxi ride booking services (ii) Restaurant to home food delivery services and (iii) Doorstep grocery delivery services.

Whoever becomes larger, has *ceteris paribus*, the lower spread and is hence the winner. New entrants can compete with the established natural monopolist, like the Consolidated did, by keeping the spread low and bearing the cost.

[9] Brown, William O., Jr., Mulherin, J. Harold and Weidenmier, Marc D., "Competing with the New York Stock Exchange," *The Quarterly Journal of Economics*, Vol. 123, No. 4, November 2008, pp. 1679–1719.

[10] Brown, William O., Jr., Mulherin, J. Harold and Weidenmier, Marc D., "Competing with the New York Stock Exchange," *The Quarterly Journal of Economics*, Vol. 123, No. 4, November 2008, pp. 1679–1719.

CHAPTER 9

Conclusions and Implications for the Evolution of Financial Markets

Abstract Summarizes the findings. Potential challengers to the New York Stock Exchange (i) conventional exchanges (ii) Platform like Bloomberg (iii) increase in technology-based trading, and the increase in direct investing by retail investors and (iii) the threat from an increase in the geographical scope of a market are discussed.

Keywords Bloomberg · Competition between exchanges · Competitive spreads · Euronext · London Stock Exchange · NASDAQ · Order book · Positive network externalities · Pre-eminent exchange · Retail investors

The dissertation on which this book is based began by collecting and analyzing price, volume, and the bid ask spread data for securities traded, in order to discover what happened to securities markets in the United States from 1830 to 1860. This was the first comprehensive quantitative analysis of stock markets for this period.

Analyzing price and volume data revealed that the NYSE began its rise to pre-eminence in 1851–1852, and this process accelerated post 1852.

The telegraph was invented and effectively demonstrated by 1844, and major cities in north-eastern US were linked by it by 1846. At this time, the NYSE was the most efficient among the exchanges under consideration, with the lowest average bid ask spread; and lower spreads that the

S. Garg, *The Telegraph and Stock Exchanges*, Palgrave Studies in Economic History, https://doi.org/10.1007/978-3-031-40407-8_9

PSE on Reading Railroad, a cross-listed security. By providing almost instantaneous communication for the first time among geographically distant points, the telegraph allowed investors the option of trading at geographically distant locations. Investors could now trade on the exchange with the lower spreads if they so wished. As the NYSE was the venue with the lowest spreads, it is logical to expect that subject to the constraint of the cost of trading via telegraph, investors in cross-listed securities would move their trades to the NYSE. The data however do not show a shift in favor of the NYSE in the late 1840s. This is because it took some years for the telegraph to become a reliable means of communication. In the early years of the telegraph, messages were often garbled due to improperly insulated wires. In addition, property rights relating to the content of the messages transmitted had to be established. Laws had to be developed to establish blame and assign punishment for incorrectly transmitted messages. All these developments took several years. Research by Tomas Nonnenmacher reveals that it took till 1852 for the telegraph to become a reliable means of communication. A survey published in 1852 reveals that the telegraph was being used to trade securities by 1851.

Though there were still issues with the reliability of the telegraph in 1851, it was being used to trade securities. Regular and extensive use of the telegraph would have begun, once the telegraph became a reliable means of communication, i.e., by 1852. Price and volume data reveal that the NYSE began its rise to pre-eminence in 1851–1852, and that this process accelerated after 1852.

As developments in transport and communications continued, more and more companies became national and were therefore often cross-listed. We assume that trade in these moved progressively to the NYSE too, further enhancing its position. The ticker tape, the transatlantic cable, and the telephone must have enhanced the position of the NYSE, further.

Competition Between Exchanges Today

The process continues today, with more and more companies becoming international or multinational in nature, and being listed on exchanges in more than one country.

Given the level of communications across the globe today the need for an international exchange, a venue to trade securities that evoke international interest is fulfilled by the NYSE.

Today, several exchanges list securities from other countries or economic regions. As of now, the NYSE, by dint of its size, and the economic size of the United States is pre-eminent among them. History also lends its weight to this preference. Even today, when a non-US-based company lists on the NYSE, it is a signal that the company is now an international one.

Current and Future Competition from Other Conventional Exchanges

Currently, the NYSE is still the largest stock exchange and the pre-eminent exchange in the world. Is there anything that can threaten this position?

The first question is about the NYSE simply being the largest exchange. The second is about the NYSE being the exchange of choice for listing "international" stocks. These are two highly interconnected questions. I will first discuss them as separate questions and then as two halves of the same.

Tables 4.1 and 4.2 have been reproduced here as Tables 9.1 and 9.2; for ease of reference.

Table 9.1 has the value of securities traded on exchanges. The value of securities (shares) traded is calculated as Price of the share x Number of shares traded.

Table 9.2 compares the size of stock exchanges based on the market capitalization of companies listed on an exchange.

Tables 9.1 and 9.2 show that the NYSE is the largest stock exchange in the world, and that the NASDAQ is the second largest. Both these are US entities. If other economies grow faster than the US economy, these economies' stock exchanges will grow too. The value of securities traded on them will grow, as will the market capitalization of companies listed on these exchanges. Though populations in China and Japan will continue to shrink in the near future, many other large Asian economies with growing populations, and increasing demand for goods and services, will have rising levels of GDP in the future. The national exchange of one of these economies, or an exchange like the Euronext, or the London Stock Exchange, may overtake the NYSE on these two metrics, in the future. Given the relative sizes of exchanges today, the possibility of this happening seems remote at present; however, the possibility does exist. Improbable but not impossible.

Table 9.1 Value of securities traded (in billions USD [$])

Largest stock exchanges worldwide as of June 2022 (by value of electronic order book share trading [in billion $])	
NYSE	3,094.23
NASDAQ US	2,197.23
Shenzhen Stock Exchange	1,883.23
Shanghai Stock Exchange	1,569.24
CBOE Global Markets	1,473.80
Japan Exchange Group	506.86
Hong Kong Exchanges and Clearing	302.86
Euronext	297.78
Korea Exchange	247.71
TMX Group	217.38
CBOE Europe	190.90
Taiwan Stock Exchange	159.60
Deutsche Boerse AG	126.94
National Stock Exchange of India	123.10
B3-Brasil Bolsa Balcao	118.85
ASX Australian Securities Exchange	106.98
London Stock Exchange	103.67

Source https://www.statista.com/statistics/270127/largest-stock-exchanges-worldwide-by-trading-volume/: Downloaded June 15, 2023

In addition to being the largest stock exchange in the world, the NYSE is also the pre-eminent exchange in the world. It is still the international venue of choice for a company that has gained "international" stature; a company that now attracts investors not just from its own country or region, but from other parts of the world too.

For the discussion on "pre-eminence," I am not considering the NASDAQ as a contender, as the NYSE and the NASDAQ largely list and trade different types of companies. Should this ever change, the NASDAQ could be a strong contender for becoming the pre-eminent international exchange.

The NYSE, besides being, or maybe because it is the largest stock exchange in the world, is also the pre-eminent exchange in the world today. The real question is whether this position of pre-eminence will continue even if it is no longer the largest exchange. Would prestige, the force of history, relationships built over time, and embedded knowledge and expertise help it retain its pre-eminent position?

Table 9.2 Market cap (in trillions USD [$])

Largest stock exchange operators worldwide as of March 2023 (by market capitalization of listed companies [in trillion $])	
NYSE, United States	25.15
NASDAQ, United States	18.99
Shanghai Stock Exchange, China	7.24
Euronext, Europe	6.72
Japan Exchange Group	5.60
Shenzhen Stock Exchange, China	5.12
Hong Kong Exchanges	4.70
National Stock Exchange of India	3.28
LSE Group, UK	3.16
TMX Group, Canada	2.92
Saudi Stock Exchange (Tadawul)	2.67
Deutsche Boerse	2.18
Nasdaq Nordic and Baltics	1.96
SIX Swiss Exchange	1.94
Korea Exchange	1.80
Tehran Stock Exchange	1.75
ASX Australian Securities Exchange	1.68
Taiwan Stock Exchange	1.63
Johannesburg Stock Exchange	1.17

Source https://www.statista.com/statistics/270126/largest-stock-exchange-operators-by-market-capitalization-of-listed-companies/: Downloaded June 19, 2023

An alternative question is: how long would the largest and the pre-eminent exchange of a region continue to be the pre-eminent exchange after it ceases being the largest exchange? Prestige, the force of history, relationships built over time, and embedded knowledge and expertise would help delay the inevitable. How long the process will take will depend on the strength of these factors. The merger of several exchanges to form Euronext and the aftermath of Brexit led to the London Stock Exchange no longer being the largest stock exchange in Europe. In the days preceding and immediately after Brexit, there was speculation about whether the knowledge and expertise and the quality of services provided by the London Stock Exchange would continue to attract non-British companies and investors.

If history is an indicator, it is only a matter of time before a pre-eminent exchange that is no longer the largest exchange, ceases to be the pre-eminent exchange.

Assuming for a moment that another exchange could become larger than the NYSE, what could hasten the process of another exchange becoming the pre-eminent exchange in the world?

There are three factors that could cause this to occur, or hasten it.

Factor 1: Even though trading in international securities now occurs 24 hours a day—with typically some or the other stock exchange being open somewhere in the world; or a platform providing off hours trading—people still prefer to trade during the day. Hence the bulk of trading on an exchange will happen during the working hours in the country where it is based. If a security is listed on more than one exchange, the exchange with the higher volume of trade will be the one with the lowest spreads; the quickest time to execution and, the lowest movement against the party initiating the trade.

Let's say Company A is currently listed on the NYSE and on Euronext. At present, the volume of trade for Company A's shares is higher on the NYSE than on Euronext. It is possible that if economies in Europe grow relatively faster than the US Economy, the volume of trade of Company A's shares on Euronext exceeds that on the NYSE. Now Euronext will become the more important venue for trading Company A's shares. If this happens for more and more companies, the Euronext may well become the exchange of choice for a newly "international" company from Asia.

Factor 2: If listing requirements become more cumbersome on the NYSE as compared to other exchanges, newly "international" companies may decide to list on an alternative international exchange such as the Euronext. Non-US companies listed on the NYSE may decide to delist from there and list on Euronext.

Factor 3: If the US Government uses permission to list and trade on the NYSE to settle political scores, companies from other countries may choose to list elsewhere.

Competition from a Platform like Bloomberg

The potential competition for being the "pre-eminent" exchange is not restricted to current traditional exchanges like the London Stock Exchange, Euronext, or the NASDAQ. Competition could come from an entity like the Bloomberg trading platform. At present, the platform is an important venue for trading Fixed Income Securities such as Treasury Bills and Bonds issued by the United States Treasury. Trading in these instruments is largely through over the counter (OTC) trading. The major traders in these instruments are central banks, institutional investors, and high net-worth individuals. The typical size of a trade is also large as compared to the typical size of a trade for traditional shares.

Given the large size of individual trades, and the relatively low frequency of trade in these instruments, entities wishing to trade sometimes break down their lot size and shop around for potential counterparties to a trade. A platform like Bloomberg facilitates these trades, by helping pool and provide information on entities offering to buy and sell each security. Information is provided on the size of the trade being offered, the bid price and the ask price.

Many of these fixed income securities are also traded on traditional exchanges, although traditional stock markets may not be the best place for getting the best prices, unlike for the trading in shares.

Information regarding the trading of these fixed income securities on traditional exchanges is also provided on Bloomberg, alongside offers to buy, and, sell from entities other than the traditional exchanges. Potential buyers and sellers have access to all this information in one place. They can make well informed decisions. This is like having access to the order book that a market maker or "specialist" has on a traditional exchange. Traditional stock markets have a bid and ask price for customers. Though Bloomberg is not a stock exchange, it lists "bid" and "ask" prices.

For five of the most frequently traded US Government issued securities, the "bid" and "ask" prices on Bloomberg, offered up by users of Bloomberg, are comparable to those listed by other entities on Bloomberg and to those being offered by traditional exchanges. The "spreads" offered up by users of Bloomberg are not the lowest, but they are comparable.

In addition to all this, Bloomberg provides its users with additional summary information if needed, and analysis regarding specific securities in which users are interested.

Using text-scraping tools to scrub chats on its network, Bloomberg is able to provide its users with even more guidance and market intelligence. As our ability to capture, store, and analyze data continues to grow, these offerings from Bloomberg will become more detailed and become quicker. This will make Bloomberg's offerings more useful.

At present, this occurs for trading in Fixed Income Securities. It is possible that this may be extended in the future to trading in shares of companies that do not have much liquidity. For final settlement for traditional securities, one will still have to go to the exchange where such securities are listed. However, as advances in communication and computing technology continue to enhance the value to be obtained from trading through the Bloomberg platform, *ceteris paribus*, trading conducted on the Bloomberg Platform will increase. This will further enhance the value of trading using Bloomberg, attracting more potential buyers and sellers. Each trade conducted using the Bloomberg Platform creates a positive network externality. The Bloomberg Platform is a natural monopoly for the same reasons that a traditional share market is a natural monopoly.

The Bloomberg Platform is already the best place to get competitive spreads for several fixed income securities. Currently, for the transfer of ownership of a security and the recording of the change of ownership of a security, one still has to go elsewhere. For example, for US Treasury bonds, one has to go to the Trustee. For the shares of a particular company, one has to go to the stock exchange on which the company has listed its shares. If regulatory changes allow a platform like Bloomberg to provide these services, or if Bloomberg could take over the responsibility of the transfer, or help facilitate, simplify, or automate the transfer, it could become a *de facto* stock exchange. Alternatively, a third party in conjunction with Bloomberg could help complete the transfer.

If changes in technology could simplify the process and reduce the cost of addressing this problem to such an extent as to render it a non-issue, there may no longer be a need for regulatory approval or change.

There has been a dramatic increase in retail investors in the last few years. For the purpose of the argument below, I divide these retail investors into two broad categories.

Category 1: These investors pick and select the shares, bonds, or indexes in which they wish to invest. They buy these by (a) getting in touch with their broker (b) using a dematerialized account or (c) using a phone-based trading application. In each instance, these investors pay the price of the share and incur other buying related costs. Such investors invest for the long term. They might often spend a lot of time researching shares and the markets.

Category 2: These investors pick and select the shares, bonds, or indexes in which they wish to invest. They buy these by (a) getting in touch with their broker (b) using a dematerialized account or (c) using a phone-based trading application. In each instance, these investors pay the price of the share and incur other buying related costs. They may or may not spend time researching shares and the markets, but they spend time buying and selling shares. Some do this for two to three hours a week. Some others may spend substantially more time than this. Many such investors are constantly watching the news and reading and listening to analyst reports; keeping up with the chatter regarding individual shares, groups of shares, and the overall market. They follow the minute by minute movement of shares, with the hope of making money in intraday trading.

Changes in communication technology such as (i) cheaper, faster, and more reliable internet connectivity and (ii) an increase in areas where the Internet is available, coupled with cheaper and better cell phones, laptops and desktops have led to an increase in both types of retail investors. A proliferation of trading applications "Apps" has helped magnify this trend.

The COVID-19 pandemic led to an increase in both types of retail investors. People had more free time on their hands as compared to before the pandemic. This was because most people could not step out of their houses, and the time they would have spent on travel, eating out, and on entertainment, and other leisure activities outside the house was now freed up. People who had jobs, saved on commute time. Some people who lost their jobs due to the pandemic found it difficult to find another job. In addition to having free time, they also needed to find a way to earn money while staying at home. Many of these people began to dabble in the stock market. What started as an interest became a full-time activity for many. The easing of pandemic related restrictions and the subsequent decrease in unemployment led to a decrease in the overall time devoted to full-time engagement with stock market related activities. Things, however, did not return to pre-pandemic levels. Among the people who had lost their jobs, some decided not to go back to conventional jobs and to continue being full-time retail investors instead. Others decided to go back to conventional jobs; many among these still devote a part of their day to active involvement in the stock market. This could mean a few hours during the work day, when the pace of work is slow.

The COVID-19 pandemic has also led to another basic change. People questioned many of their long-held beliefs. As a result of large-scale lay-offs, they lost faith in the idea that working diligently at a conventional job provided security. They realized that life is inherently uncertain. As a result, they became less risk averse. People began to prioritize their own well-being over the requirements of a conventional job. People also realized that they could live with much less money than they had imagined. All these changes led to people choosing to work for themselves, and not for others. Those that chose to work for others began to prefer part-time work, rather than a full-time job. These people now have much more free time on their hands. Many choose to spend this free time as Category 2 "retail investors."

Trading by mutual funds, banks, pension funds, and high net-worth individuals is often in large lot sizes. Such trades can have a considerable impact on the market. These trades are closely watched, monitored, and analyzed. The ability to predict such trades and their impact can help predict the future movement of markets.

At any given moment in time on a stock exchange, there is a bid and an ask price for each security. Entities that wish to trade at these prices, do so, subject to the availability of enough shares to be sold, or enough demand by potential buyers. In addition to orders being completed at the current bid ask spread, there are other orders that are waiting in line, hoping for a higher bid price or a lower ask price. These constitute the "order book." Information in the "order book" can help predict which way the market will move.

Market makers and specialists on stock markets have access to knowledge of not just the orders that are being executed, but also to the order book. Anyone privy to the information in the order book has a better idea of the way the market is going to move, as compared to someone who does not. Bloomberg displays the offers to buy and sell. Users in effect have access to the order book.

At present, the Bloomberg Platform does not list securities. All it does is display offers to buy and sell. Entities get in touch with each other on the basis of these offers to buy and sell. The entities then directly trade with each other. The responsibility for the transfer of ownership of a security and for the recording of the change of ownership is the responsibility of these entities. Bloomberg only provides the platform for them to meet and exchange information.

In a traditional exchange, a broker collects the orders from retail investors and helps them execute these orders. The information regarding the "order book" for these trades is with the broker. On a platform like Bloomberg, large entities trade with each other. The final execution of these trades (the delivery of the asset, and the recording of change of ownership) remains the responsibility of the trading entities. Large entities can do this cost effectively for themselves. The cost per trade for doing this is very high for retail investors, hence they continue to go through their banks or brokers. If a platform like Bloomberg in addition to facilitating potential buyers and sellers get information about each other, also helped in the delivery of the asset once a trade is executed, and in the recording of change of ownership, and if this service was provided at competitive prices, it would attract a lot of the retail investor trades. Given the large number of retail investors, these services could be provided at competitive prices. The "order book" of even more retail investment trades would then be available to everyone on the platform.

People are becoming more tech savvy. People are also taking a more hands-on approach to managing their own investments. These trends will lead to an increase in retail investing.

The pooling of retail investment data, added to the trading data of large buyers and sellers on a platform like Bloomberg, can be a game changer. Changes in technology, such as text-scraping tools that glean information from online chats on a platform and pool and share this information with users on the platform, will help enhance the value of being a part of such a network.

Conventional exchanges will have to decide whether to treat these changes as a threat to their conventional setup, where knowledge of the order book is with the market maker on the exchange. Sharing this information in real time with others will mean sharing this advantage. If sharing this attracts retail investors away from a platform like Bloomberg, conventional exchanges will have to weigh the costs and benefits of doing so.

Technological Changes that Increase the Geographical Scope of a Market

Even with the current level of communications technology, *ceteris paribus* people still prefer to first invest close to where they live.[1] In part, this is because of the trust factor. A person living in Country D might wish to invest in shares of a company listed on the national exchange of Country

[1] Once people have invested a certain amount close to home, some may venture out to invest in assets in remoter geographical locations, in a bid to geographically diversify their portfolio.

E. She might choose not to, if she is worried that if something goes wrong, she would not be able to do anything about it; or if she could, it would not be worth the time and effort.

Innovations like block chain technology, by reducing the probability of some types of fraud, help overcome trust related concerns to some extent. To the extent that these technological changes are incorporated into the buying and selling of shares, investing will become more international as compared to today.

As it becomes easier to invest remotely, conventional exchanges across the world will be brought into closer competition with each other. Although the physical locations of exchanges, the companies that they list, and the people who choose to invest in them remain unchanged, exchanges that were essentially operating as largely separate markets, will be brought into competition with each other. Just like when the telegraph brought the NYSE, the Boston Stock Exchange, and the Philadelphia Stock Exchange into competition with each other, in the present day too, the most "efficient" exchange should win, at the cost of the others.

CHAPTER 10

What the Telegraph Can Teach Us About Uber

Abstract Extends the learnings from the competition between stock exchanges to competition between (i) car rental aggregator services such as Uber and Ola (iii) restaurant to home, food delivery services such as Zomato and Swiggy and (iii) doorstep delivery services such as Blinkit and Zepto.

Keywords Bid ask spreads · Blinkit and Zepto · Economies of scale · Contestable Monopoly · Natural duopoly · Natural monopoly · Positive network externalities · Swiggy and Zomato · Uber and Ola · Wait time for booked taxi to arrive · Indrive

Natural Monopolies

Stock markets have positive network externalities, which leads to economies of scale. So do taxi ride booking services like Uber and Ola. Whoever becomes larger, *ceteris paribus*, has the lower cost per unit of service provided. Being large brings down costs per unit and gives you an advantage.

You could also reverse the causation; a company could lower the price charged per unit, gain customers/market share, and grow large. Growing in size leads to costs going down, and to even more customers. This is

S. Garg, *The Telegraph and Stock Exchanges*, Palgrave Studies in Economic History, https://doi.org/10.1007/978-3-031-40407-8_10

what Ola, Uber, Swiggy, and Zomato did; and what Blinkit and Zepto are doing at present.

Taxi ride booking services like Uber and Ola (an Indian company offering an Application "App" and services similar to Uber) experience positive network externalities, and hence *inter alia* have economies of scale. As the number of rides booked rises, the fixed costs of the firm are spread over a larger number of rides booked. The firm can then choose to pass on these lower costs to (i) riders, by charging them a lower price per ride (ii) drivers, by letting them retain a larger portion of the amount charged to the customer or both (i) and (ii).

Lower prices will lead to more customers both signing up for Uber and booking rides using the Uber App. Higher payments to drivers will lead to more drivers joining the Uber network and providing services via the Uber App to the Uber network.

Each new potential rider and new driver that joins, signs up, and uses the Uber App creates a positive "network externality." Riders want to book through an App that has more drivers, as this means a shorter wait to find a driver. Drivers want to be associated with an App that has more potential riders, as the time to find a ride reduces as the number of potential riders rises. The distance a driver has to travel to get to the next ride also reduces as the number of potential riders booking through the App rises.

More potential riders lead to more drivers, and more drivers lead to more potential riders. Both these lead to more rides being booked. An increase in the number of rides being booked leads to a further reduction in the fixed costs per ride.

This market has positive network externalities which lead to economies of scale. In a market left to itself, one firm will become the dominant firm. This firm is a "natural monopoly."

In certain cases, if the size of the market is large enough, there is scope for two natural monopolists to exist. The market is so large that more than one firm can become large enough to achieve effective economies of scale. This is a situation of a "natural duopoly."

Can This Position of a "Natural Monopoly" Be Challenged?

A ride booking App like Uber operates in the following way. Potential riders and drivers sign up to the App. Once a ride is booked and completed using the App, the rider pays for the ride. The rider either pays Uber or pays the driver directly. If the rider has paid Uber, Uber retains a portion of the amount paid and transfers the rest to the driver. If the rider pays the driver directly, Uber adjusts its cut against the amount owed to the driver for other rides; essentially rides where the rider paid Uber directly. Sometimes, if many or all the riders during a particular time slot have paid the driver directly, the driver may have to transfer Uber's cut to Uber, before the driver gets any more bookings through the Uber App.

The difference between what the rider pays and what the driver receives can be thought of as Uber's spread. Uber is in effect buying the service from the driver, by bidding for the service. This can be considered the "Bid Price." Uber is in effect selling the service to the rider, asking for a certain price for the service. This can be considered the "Ask Price." The difference between the two (Ask Price–Bid Price), the bid ask spread is the payment to Uber for providing the services of the App.

How is this bid ask spread used to (i) establish oneself in a market where the service one wishes to provide simply does not exist (ii) enter a market where there is already an established "natural monopolist" providing the very service you wish to provide or (iii) prevent the entry of a potential rival?

Let us take an example. Company Z wants to enter and establish itself in a market where it believes there are positive network externalities, and there exists the potential for becoming a natural monopolist. Let us say that this is a company that helps drivers and potential riders connect and book rides. Company Z offers customers very low introductory prices, lower than the actual cost of providing the taxi ride. At the same time, it offers the driver an amount higher than what it receives from the customer. This amount could be substantially higher than the cost of providing the ride.

As a result, both customers and drivers sign up. Then the network externalities operate as explained above. Once Company Z believes it has become the "natural monopolist" it begins to lower the incentives to both riders and drivers. If Company Z feels that its monopoly position cannot be challenged, it can start charging customers prices higher than the cost of providing the ride, hoping that customers may (i) not notice, or if they do notice they (ii) continue to book through the App, because of the convenience, and because of the lack of alternatives. Company Z can start lowering the amount paid to drivers, hoping that drivers will not leave the network because of the convenience that the App provides.

Company Z can now enjoy high bid ask spreads.

Uber and Ola

Uber and Ola are two Taxi Service Aggregators that operate in New Delhi.[1]

Anecdotal evidence reveals that when Uber company started operations in New Delhi, India, it charged customers prices that were lower than what customers would have had to pay for a ride in a taxi they had booked directly. Uber paid the driver practically the entire amount it received from customers. Anecdotal evidence suggests that Uber also gave drivers additional incentives and bonuses. These incentives and bonuses led to a surge in the number of people joining the Uber network as drivers.[2]

Anecdotal evidence shows that when it first started operations in New Delhi, Uber deliberately operated with low and, some suggest even negative spreads. This was done to gain market share. As of June 2023, anecdotal evidence suggests that it has very large spreads. The analysis is similar for Ola.[3]

Are these spreads large enough to create the space for a competitor to enter, i.e., attract a competitor? A competitor in a city so large that the competitor can also achieve very low average costs before the increasing returns to scale are exhausted?

[1] The analysis is presented for Uber, as I have personally collected anecdotal evidence regarding Uber. The same analysis applies to Ola.

[2] Uber paid drivers a lot (high "bid" prices) and charged customers very low prices (low "ask" prices). Uber initially operated with very low spreads; back of the envelope calculations based on anecdotal evidence suggests that Uber was overall paying drivers more than Uber was collecting from riders, i.e.; "ask" prices lower than "bid" prices; i.e.; negative spreads.

[3] At one time Ola and Uber were the "natural duopolists" in this market. Ola was severely affected by the COVID-19 pandemic. It is still operational in New Delhi. Whether or not it is a viable challenger to Uber, depends upon whom one talks to. I have collected data in person, only regarding Uber.

An important consideration when choosing a taxi booking App is the time it takes for the booked taxi to arrive. The variance in the time it takes for a booked taxi to arrive is also important. The lower the variance the better. A rider will choose to book through an App that has a 5 minute wait time, each time she books a ride; as compared to an App which may have a wait time of 3 minutes in one instance and 14 minutes in another instance. *Ceteris paribus,* as the number of riders booking through an App, and the number of drivers providing rides booked through an App increase, the variance in wait time also reduces.

Table 10.1 and Graph 10.1 illustrate how the time it takes for a booked taxi to arrive, reduces as the number of riders using a particular App increase. These data are hypothetical and are presented with the aim of illustrating the concept of a contestable monopoly. The data are for when one books a taxi at a busy marketplace.

The number of riders and the number of drivers are inter dependent. An increase in one leads to an increase in the other. The higher the number of riders, the lower the wait time for a booked taxi to arrive. I have assumed that a wait time of a minute is low enough, and that any further reductions in this do not affect the choice of a booking App.

Graph 10.2 presents the same data as Graph 10.1, in an alternative format.

Graph 10.3 presents partial data from Table 10.1. Data are for wait times less than a minute.

Let us start with one App provider in the market. The size of the market is 1,200,000 riders. If all the riders in this market book taxis through this App, the number of riders is 1,200,000 (corresponding to X on Table 10.1 and Graphs 10.1–10.3), and the wait time is 0.46 minutes. A new App provider enters the market. I am assuming that it is easier for the existing App provider to retain a customer, than it is for a new entrant to attract a customer. I am also assuming that if the new entrant manages to attract riders and drivers by providing incentives to both, the existing firm will also make an effort to retain riders and drivers.

If the new entrant manages to attract and retain up to 550,000 riders (corresponding to K on Table 10.1 and Graphs 10.1–10.3), the wait time for booking through its App is 0.98 minutes. The original App provider now has only 650,000 riders (corresponding to M on Table 10.1 and Graphs 10.1–10.3), and the wait time for booking through its App rises to 0.9 minutes. Though the wait time of 0.9 minutes is lower than the

Table 10.1 Wait time (in minutes) for a booked Taxi to arrive to pick up the rider (at a busy marketplace)

	Number of riders signed up for, and using the App	*Wait time (in minutes) for a booked taxi to arrive to pick up the rider (at a busy marketplace)*
A	50,000	156
B	100,000	116
C	150,000	78
D	200,000	58
E	250,000	42
F	300,000	26
G	350,000	16
H	400,000	8
I	450,000	4
J	500,000	2
K	550,000	0.98
L	600,000	0.94
M	650,000	0.9
N	700,000	0.86
O	750,000	0.82
P	800,000	0.78
Q	850,000	0.74
R	900,000	0.7
S	950,000	0.66
T	1,000,000	0.62
U	1,050,000	0.58
V	1,100,000	0.54
W	1,150,000	0.5
X	1,200,000	0.46

wait time of 0.98 minutes, both are below 1 minute, and hence will not affect the choice of Apps.

Hence if the provider of the new App can get even less than half the market share, it can effectively compete on the basis of wait time. This is an example of a contestable monopoly.

If the number of potential riders in this market was 1,800,000 instead of 1,200,000 three App providers could enter the market and compete on the basis of wait time.

Markets with lower number of riders may not be contestable markets. Let us start with a smaller market; a market that has only 600,000 potential riders instead of 1,200,000. There is one company that provides

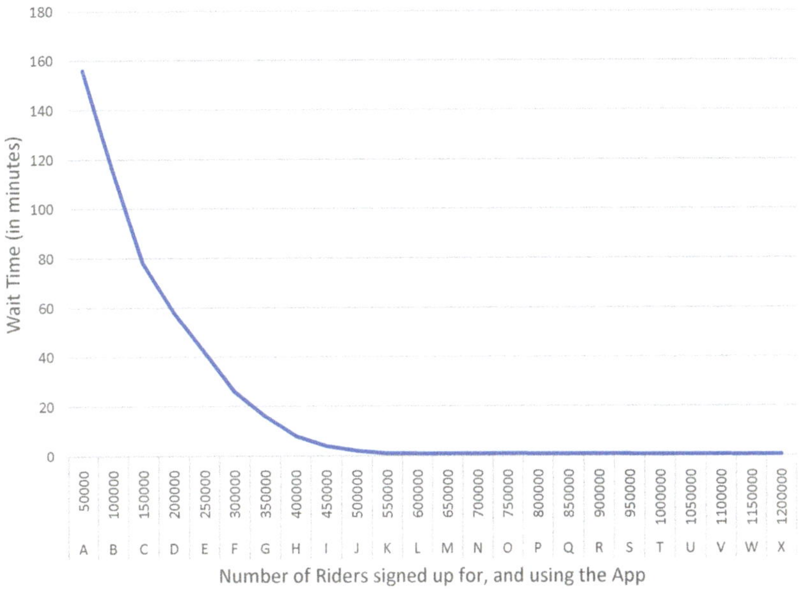

Graph 10.1 Wait time (in minutes) for a booked taxi to arrive to pick up the rider (at a busy marketplace)

an App for booking taxi rides. All the riders in this market book taxis through this App. The number of riders is 600,000 (corresponding to L on Table 10.1 and Graphs 10.1–10.3), and the wait time is 0.94 minutes. I assume that it is easier for an existing App provider to retain a rider than it is for a new App provider to attract a rider. A new App provider attracts 250,000 riders (corresponding to E on Table 10.1 and Graphs 10.1 and 10.2), the wait time for booking through its App is 42 minutes. The original App provider now has only 350,000 riders (corresponding to G on Table 10.1 and Graphs 10.1 and 10.2), and the wait time for booking through its App rises to 16 minutes. The new App provider will not be able to compete on the basis of wait time, i.e., the original App provider's position as a natural monopolist would be difficult to contest on the basis of wait time.

Table 10.1 and Graphs 10.1–10.3 have data on wait time at a busy marketplace. One minute of wait time is considered as low enough in such a situation. Such a low wait time may be unrealistic in other situations.

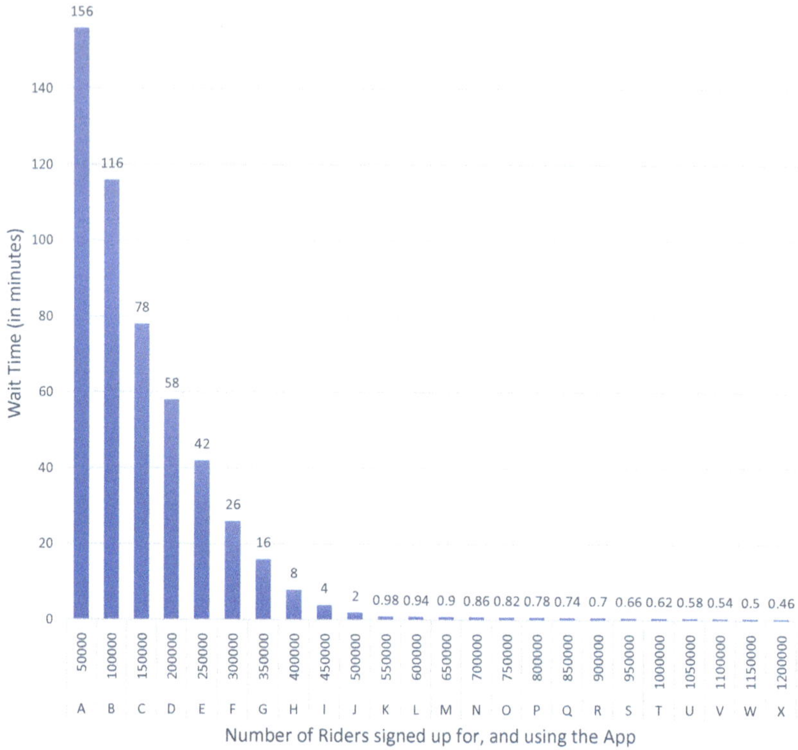

Graph 10.2 Wait time (in minutes) for a booked taxi to arrive to pick up the rider (at a busy marketplace)

Table 10.2 and Graph 10.4 have data on wait times when one books a taxi from a residential area. I have assumed that a wait time of three minutes is low enough, and that any further reductions in this do not affect the choice of a booking App.

There is at least one new contender that has entered the market in New Delhi, India.

Indrive, a ride booking App that allows potential riders and drivers to negotiate prices is gaining market share in New Delhi, India. Anecdotal evidence suggests that many drivers are switching, or planning to switch to Indrive in the near future. Riders too are downloading the App and recommending it to friends. It will be interesting to watch,

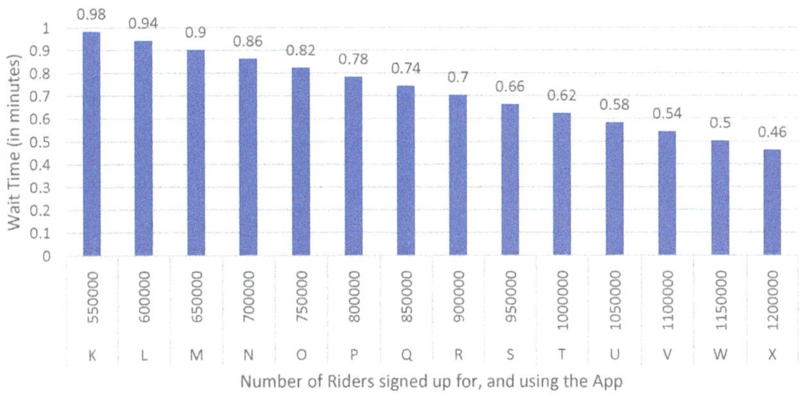

Graph 10.3 Wait time (in minutes) for a booked taxi to arrive to pick up the rider (at a busy marketplace) (partial data from Table 10.1)

if Uber will lower its current high "bid-ask spreads" (high based on anecdotal evidence) to retain current drivers and riders. It might start a "price war" to maintain its market share. It might even lower spreads to such an extent, that the newer entrant will face losses if it matches those spreads. Uber may even lower spreads so much that Uber itself also faces losses; in the hope that the newer entrant will have to lower its spreads below Uber's in order to attract drivers and riders. If such spreads are loss making for Uber, they will be even more loss making, per unit of service provided, for the newer entrant. At present, as Uber has a larger network than Indrive, its total losses may be higher, the same, or lower than Indrive. If loss making spreads are charged by both Uber and Indrive, the last App standing may be the one whose backers have the ability and willingness to incur larger losses and/or losses for longer.

Uber could instead keep spreads as they are, and ride it out. This would mean accommodating one or more newer rivals. It is also possible that Uber's currently high bid ask spreads are an indication that it plans to make as much money as possible, till as long as it can, and then, when other competitors enter, either exit the market or let the App continue earning whatever reduced amount it does. New Delhi will watch this competition with interest.

The market is large enough that the current natural monopolist's position is not that of a "natural monopoly;" but rather a "natural duopoly."

Table 10.2 Wait time (in minutes) for a booked taxi to arrive to pick up the rider (at a residential area)

Number of riders signed up for, and using the App	*Wait time (in minutes)*
50,000	158
100,000	118
150,000	80
200,000	60
250,000	44
300,000	28
350,000	18
400,000	10
450,000	6
500,000	4
550,000	2.8
600,000	2.6
650,000	2.4
700,000	2.2
750,000	2
800,000	1.85
850,000	1.75
900,000	1.65
950,000	1.55
1,000,000	1.45
1,050,000	1.35
1,100,000	1.25
1,150,000	1.15
1,200,000	1.05

Given the size of the market, a new entrant can exhaust, or come close to exhausting the economies of scale, even in the presence of another established large firm, even when the established firm is so large that it too has exhausted, or come close to exhausting the economies of scale.

Given the size of the taxi ride market in New Delhi India, the existing "natural monopoly[4]" is a contestable monopoly.

[4] Or "natural duopoly" depending on whom you talk to.

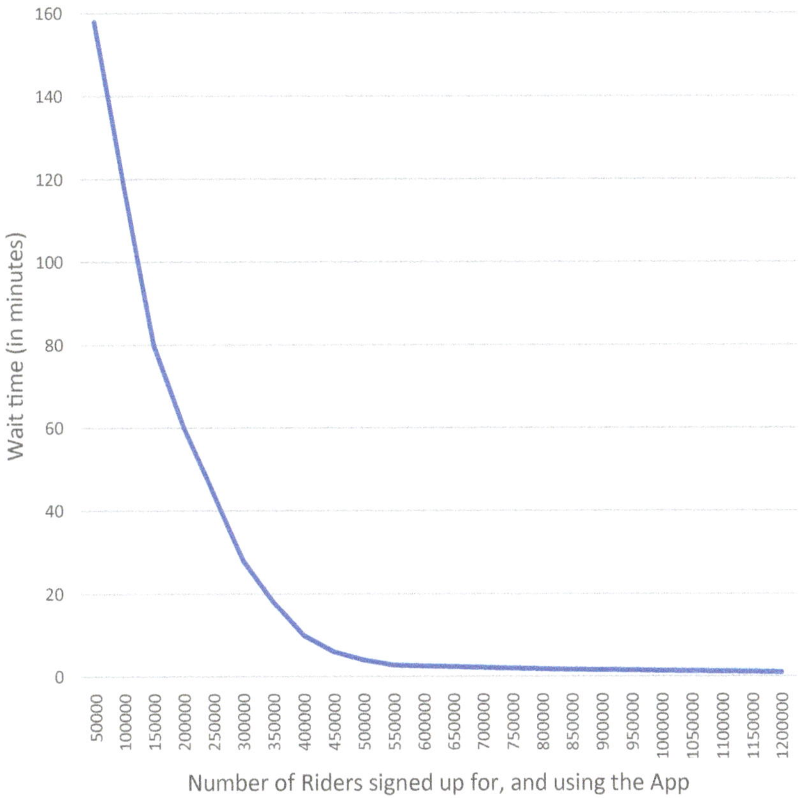

Graph 10.4 Wait time (in minutes) for a booked taxi to arrive to pick up the rider (at a residential area)

Swiggy and Zomato

Swiggy and Zomato are food delivery Apps. They help consumers connect to restaurants, order food from the restaurants, and have the food delivered to the home of the customer.[5] Apps such as Swiggy and Zomato also have positive network externalities which lead, *inter alia* to economies of scale. The analysis and explanation are analogous to that for taxi ride aggregators and so are not repeated here.

[5] Uber Eats and Grubhub provide similar services in New York City.

Swiggy and Zomato also started with low spreads and incentivized users to sign up. Anecdotal evidence suggests that they too increased their spreads once they had gained a certain amount of market share. This market also has the characteristics of a natural duopoly. Given the current high spreads the market is ripe for a new entrant. The options open to Swiggy and Zomato, when responding to a new entrant, are similar to Uber's.

Blinkit and Zepto

Blinkit and Zepto are two doorstep delivery services that deliver goods at very short notice. These services are still in their nascent stage in New Delhi, India. There are many firms providing the same service, each of whom is currently charging low spreads to gain market share. These services also have positive network externalities which *inter alia*, lead to economies of scale. Given the size of the potential market for such services in New Delhi, two or more natural monopolists should emerge as the winners.

CHAPTER 11

Antitrust Policy: To Intervene or To Not Intervene—That Is the Question

Abstract Discusses the competition between natural monopolies and the antitrust policy implications when a natural monopoly is a contestable natural monopoly and when the natural monopoly is non contestable. The policy recommendation is that if the natural monopoly is a contestable monopoly, then, even when the natural monopoly is charging prices significantly higher than they could have charged if there were competitors, regulators need not intervene. The market, left to itself, will eventually give the desired outcome. If the natural monopoly is not a contestable monopoly, and the natural monopolist is charging prices much higher than could have been charged if there were competitors, then the antitrust regulators must intervene. They could, for example, regulate the natural monopoly in a manner similar to how public utilities are regulated.

Keywords Antitrust · Competition between exchanges · Contestable monopoly · Economies of scale · Economies of scope · Natural monopoly · Non-contestable monopoly · Positive network externalities · Public Utility · Regulation of natural monopolies

S. Garg, *The Telegraph and Stock Exchanges*, Palgrave Studies in Economic History, https://doi.org/10.1007/978-3-031-40407-8_11

Aside from the markets studied in this book, the provision of many public utilities such as water and electricity supply to households within a city are also natural monopolies. *Ceteris paribus*, the lower the competition, the higher the prices charged to customers. One way to circumvent this is to have more than one supplier of the service; to have for example two or more companies supplying electricity to a neighborhood. This is wasteful from a resource usage point of view.

Regulation of Natural Monopolies

To prevent the possibility of relatively higher prices being charged by such a natural monopolist, as compared to those that would be charged in a situation where there is more than one supplier; such services are either provided by the government or the prices these natural monopolists can charge are regulated by the government.

Should the natural monopolies study in this book: stock exchanges, taxi booking services, restaurant to home delivery services, and doorstep delivery services be regulated like the provision of public utilities like water and electricity?

Some natural monopolies are contestable monopolies. The market is so large that even after the natural monopolist has taken over the entire market and achieved very low costs because of economies of scale, a competitor can enter the market; and achieve costs low enough to compete with the incumbent.

For example, once an application-based taxi booking service becomes a monopolist and starts pricing accordingly, should the government intervene in the market to ensure more competitive prices? If the natural monopoly is a contestable monopoly, the market left to itself will eventually ensure a movement toward more competitive prices. If the natural monopolist charges high enough prices, new firms will enter the market and achieve economies of scale adequate to effectively compete with the existing natural monopolist. The market left to itself ensures the desired outcome, and the government does not need to intervene.

For a contestable monopoly, if the natural monopolist, recognizing the contestable nature of its monopoly position, and wishing to reduce the incentive for competitors to enter, charges prices lower than it could charge, given its monopoly position; then in this scenario too, the market left to itself ensures the desired outcome, and the government does not need to intervene.

If the existing firms are using anti-competitive methods to prevent entry, such as intimidating potential entrants by using strong arm techniques against the app providers or their drivers, antitrust regulators must intervene. When markets are contestable, antitrust authorities should ensure that competitive forces are given full play. Then, the market, left to itself will ensure more competitive prices and spreads, as compared to monopoly prices and spreads.

If the market is non contestable, if for example, the size of the potential market is so small that once a single firm has taken over the entire market, a new entrant will not be able to attract enough customers to achieve adequate economies of scale; then the government should intervene. Potential competitors will not be able to enter and compete effectively, and hence the market left to itself will not ensure the desired outcome.

Stock markets have economies of scale, economies of scope, and positive network externalities.

Economies of scope occur because *ceteris paribus* companies wish to list where other companies are listing and because investors find it more convenient to buy and sell their shares from a particular region on a single stock exchange, as compared to dealing with several exchanges. An increase in the number of securities listed on a stock exchange leads to more companies wishing to, and listing on this stock exchange.

Given (i) positive network externalities, and economies of scale and scope in stock markets (ii) that ceteris paribus people prefer to invest nearer home and (iii) that ceteris paribus the level of economic activity in a region influences the size of stock markets; once a stock market becomes the pre-eminent exchange for a region, i.e., the natural monopolist, and the economic activity in the region remains high in absolute and relative terms; then this stock market finds it easier to retain its natural monopoly position. Is this of concern to regulators? Should they intervene?

Though a region's pre-eminent stock exchange's position as a natural monopoly may not be as quickly contestable as compared to for example the market for application-based taxi bookings in a large enough market, the pre-eminent stock market of a region faces a lot of actual and potential competition. There is a lot of internal competition; i.e., competition from within a stock market. This helps to keep bid ask spreads low. From a regulatory perspective, this is a desirable outcome.

In a region with a pre-eminent stock exchange, new stock exchanges can be set up; which can then trade in some of the securities traded on the pre-eminent exchange. This is what happened with the NYSE and the Consolidated Exchange. Spreads on the pre-eminent exchange, the NYSE, fell during the time these two exchanges competed. Though the Consolidated Exchange ceased operations, the potential of such competition can help keep spreads lower than they would be if there was no possibility of potential entrants. This too is a desirable outcome from a regulatory perspective.

Given the global nature of investors and companies, stock markets are contestable natural monopolies. The NYSE, today's pre-eminent international exchange faces challenges to this position from national exchanges and to a larger extent pre-eminent stock exchanges of economic regions across the globe. This encourages innovation, which is yet another desirable outcome from a regulatory perspective.

As long as pre-eminent exchanges have adequate internal competition and take into account the ever-present potential for competition, antitrust regulators need not intervene in these markets. The contestable nature of these natural monopolies will help ensure the desirable outcome from a competition perspective.

Appendix A: Value of Securities Traded on Each Exchange

Value of securities traded on each exchange (in USD) ($)

	Year	*NYSE*	*Philadelphia*	*Boston*
Aug	1832	37,602.5	914.4166667	
Sep	1832	52,533.75	2165.125	
Oct	1832	119,760	3213.833333	
Nov	1832	547,661	3287.125	
Dec	1832	104,954.25	3256.583333	
Jan	1833		3870.541667	
Feb	1833		3969.25	
Mar	1833		22,475.3125	
Apr	1833		15,411.5	
May	1833		9725	
Jun	1833		36,192.75	
Jul	1833		13,287	
Aug	1833		78,449	
Sep	1833		70,370.25	
Oct	1833		4327.25	
Nov	1833		35,213	
Dec	1833		10,220	
Jan	1834	307,611	7806	
Feb	1834	159,776	9538.5	
Mar	1834	80,541.25	12,808.5	
Apr	1834	232,851.5	19,438.125	
May	1834	213,782.5	9205.875	

(continued)

S. Garg, *The Telegraph and Stock Exchanges*, Palgrave Studies in Economic History, https://doi.org/10.1007/978-3-031-40407-8

(continued)

Value of securities traded on each exchange (in USD) ($)				
	Year	*NYSE*	*Philadelphia*	*Boston*
Jun	1834	282,442	10,863.25	
Jul	1834	400,164.25	2782.25	
Aug	1834	376,899.75	27,323.75	
Sep	1834	400,192.75	35,671.5	
Oct	1834		38,969.5	
Nov	1834		34,115.75	
Dec	1834		13,501.5	
Jan	1835		29,368.25	
Feb	1835	926,204	62,580.5	
Mar	1835	696,819	117,777	
Apr	1835	1,285,734.75	183,473.125	
May	1835	1,070,456.75	278,943.375	
Jun	1835		20,484.25	
Jul	1835		29,620.66667	31,554
Aug	1835		17,937.33333	37,026.375
Sep	1835		8598.25	5872.75
Oct	1835		112,170.5	28,454.5
Nov	1835		135,200.375	
Dec	1835		121,188.5	
Jan	1836		142,914	11,548.25
Feb	1836		239,484.75	29,681.5
Mar	1836		117,398	27,191.5
Apr	1836		131,867.5	9255.875
May	1836	527,441.25	124,888	16,253.75
Jun	1836	545,789	88,992.5	94,259
Jul	1836	308,479	96,477	
Aug	1836	581,964.5	133,034.5	
Sep	1836	460,990.25	110,788.5	
Oct	1836	428,597.75	62,625	
Nov	1836	459,723	94,702	
Dec	1836	297,381.25	42,635	
Jan	1837	556,455.5	153,875.75	
Feb	1837	426,795.5	109,678.25	
Mar	1837	297,174	99,109.5	
Apr	1837	137,359	10,055	
May	1837	75,103	4485.5	
Jun	1837	63,220.125	5084	
Jul	1837	76,023.5	11,244	
Aug	1837	177,769.5	1148	
Sep	1837	104,535.125	5763	

(continued)

(continued)

Value of securities traded on each exchange (in USD) ($)

	Year	*NYSE*	*Philadelphia*	*Boston*
Oct	1837	129,572.875	18,404.2	
Nov	1837	116,846.25	71,131	
Dec	1837	150,352.5	8449.5	
Jan	1838	97,985.375	29,354	
Feb	1838	112,161.875	18,465	
Mar	1838	74,279.5	2861.5	
Apr	1838	129,706.5	30,476.25	
May	1838	388,590.25	54,488.25	
Jun	1838	408,477.75	55,634.5	
Jul	1838	282,771.25	16,314.5	
Aug	1838	289,916	12,635	
Sep	1838	449,257.75	20,224.25	
Oct	1838	400,363.5	24,599.5	
Nov	1838	285,465.75	48,470.5	
Dec	1838	168,037.375	6621.75	
Jan	1839	396,742	21,834.25	24,932.25
Feb	1839	695,492.25	18,094.25	38,765
Mar	1839	334,775	36,773	
Apr	1839	459,067	25,581.75	
May	1839	181,493	30,512.5	
Jun	1839	164,348	19,254	3688.25
Jul	1839	173,692	25,552	7942
Aug	1839	280,748	39,272.75	5822
Sep	1839	212,796	24,718.125	20,296
Oct	1839	169,019	54,654.5	3553
Nov	1839	165,687	15,843	5555
Dec	1839	386,453	9380	1455
Jan	1840	212,241	14,728.5	10,630.5
Feb	1840	240,304	42,940	23,623
Mar	1840	204,110	24,393.5	26,509.25
Apr	1840	137,250	23,555.25	15,449
May	1840	158,209	5624.75	13,886.875
Jun	1840	149,418	22,227.25	39,356
Jul	1840	293,085	10,355.25	12,464.125
Aug	1840	97,917	21,259.5	
Sep	1840	203,762	30,769.25	19,129.75
Oct	1840	341,840	7190.25	18,011.25
Nov	1840	252,481	43,470	21,891.75
Dec	1840	288,337	206,438	14,842
Jan	1841	299,942.875		11,281.625

(continued)

(continued)

Value of securities traded on each exchange (in USD) ($)				
	Year	*NYSE*	*Philadelphia*	*Boston*
Feb	1841	170,492.5	16,533	7795
Mar	1841	74,172.5	10,763.3333	17,494.25
Apr	1841	54,650.25	15,518.6429	19,695.25
May	1841	167,765	12,688.4722	9346.3
Jun	1841	119,027.5	7293.85714	2857.5
Jul	1841	58,009.875	5380.52083	8363.95
Aug	1841	95,733.5	9206.41667	6044.875
Sep	1841	123,272.5	13,488.5417	18,065.75
Oct	1841	68,278.75	6686.25	6619
Nov	1841	189,281	14,593.875	7159
Dec	1841	149,113.125	11,691.8	12,253.5
Jan	1842	183,129	10,727.2	15,024.25
Feb	1842	92,340	7681.33333	4496.75
Mar	1842	123,375	1426.85714	8479.25
Apr	1842	113,548	4540	16,238
May	1842	100,133	4540.16667	17,859
Jun	1842	55,700	4696.66667	20,214.63
Jul	1842	53,816.25	2848.2	7799.7
Aug	1842	59,387.75	1209.33333	8218.25
Sep	1842	61,565	3161.75	31,993.45
Oct	1842	18,827	7615	5882.5
Nov	1842	38,135	3548.625	7025
Dec	1842	75,885	2183.7	8922
Jan	1843	96,448.5	4991.95	
Feb	1843	77,447.5	7811.79167	
Mar	1843	74,948	5537.75	
Apr	1843	106,738	17,661	
May	1843	402,098.5	92,252	
Jun	1843	166,756	27,061	
Jul	1843	55,383.75	13,317.75	
Aug	1843	66,713	27,250.7083	
Sep	1843	201,230.5	59,875.75	
Oct	1843	131,943.75	71,811.75	18,268.625
Nov	1843	331,090.5	58,293	
Dec	1843	460,121	53,620.25	23,962.375
Jan	1844	228,206.5	43,729.25	36,790.25
Feb	1844	539,537.75	43,860	30,668.625
Mar	1844	313,543.75	96,034.875	13,558.5
Apr	1844	392,763.5	48,231.75	11,984.875
May	1844	418,688.25	86,047	46,041.75

(continued)

(continued)

Value of securities traded on each exchange (in USD) ($)				
	Year	*NYSE*	*Philadelphia*	*Boston*
Jun	1844	231,000.5	23,173	33,263.75
Jul	1844	190,248.75	23,953	29,699.5
Aug	1844	363,173	25,868.75	123,224.88
Sep	1844	189,626.38	46,179	57,173.125
Oct	1844	194,587.5	27,815	48,280.75
Nov	1844	340,675	55,687.5	11,406.75
Dec	1844	192,403.75	53,870.75	9403.125
Jan	1845	202,599.5	152,632.5	16,486.125
Feb	1845	389,481	54,975	24,929.5
Mar	1845	198,970.63	132,123.88	25,911.125
Apr	1845	297,176.5	108,988.25	29,855.75
May	1845	204,596.88	37,550	19,491.75
Jun	1845	173,872.75	50,164.25	119,046.5
Jul	1845	160,600	70,777.125	49,282.375
Aug	1845	225,155.88	22,144	131,861.75
Sep	1845	301,993.75	78,481	181,560.38
Oct	1845	230,739.75	40,925.75	96,617.75
Nov	1845	471,065.88	41,310	103,814.5
Dec	1845	297,270.5	141,244.75	112,116.13
Jan	1846	213,375	87,506	63,997.875
Feb	1846	241,779.25	75,279.375	57,957.5
Mar	1846	207,873	31,940.625	38,471.25
Apr	1846	359,006	28,803	16,880.75
May	1846	163,048	55,130.25	33,860
Jun	1846	191,367	27,397	11,293.75
Jul	1846	136,028	56,896	33,856
Aug	1846	276,050	19,478.5	592.5
Sep	1846	212,487	6642	22,212.51
Oct	1846	231,819	8465	25,389.625
Nov	1846	172,319	8546.75	14,182.5
Dec	1846	191,405	21,475.25	8211.75
Jan	1847	429,947	52,014.75	20,420.625
Feb	1847	291,663	90,833	21,642.125
Mar	1847	148,423	28,984	45,660.25
Apr	1847	323,568	103,895.75	2595.625
May	1847	240,917.5	78,521	28,193.75
Jun	1847	203,368	163,097.75	57,819.5
Jul	1847	371,585	33,882.5	36,603.625
Aug	1847	354,375.63	57,495	46,814.5
Sep	1847	199,296.25	33,804.75	14,182.875

(continued)

(continued)

Value of securities traded on each exchange (in USD) ($)				
	Year	*NYSE*	*Philadelphia*	*Boston*
Oct	1847	391,490.63	72,930	79,628
Nov	1847	351,836.88	75,185	12,638.125
Dec	1847	290,795	42,370	123,513.25
Jan	1848	329,811.63	58,728	26,692.375
Feb	1848	205,159.18	59,871.75	52,821.5
Mar	1848	357,288.63	51,940	28,147.75
Apr	1848	378,080.63	12,528	24,942.75
May	1848	162,406.38	37,005.25	207,153.63
Jun	1848	176,518.75	54,456	22,585
Jul	1848	92,159.375	36,400	6967.375
Aug	1848	146,950.25	18,760	7031.25
Sep	1848	185,801.13	19,270	10,970.25
Oct	1848		18,607	6017
Nov	1848	215,861.13	22,833.25	62,190.875
Dec	1848	376,169.63	37,944.5	7648.75
Jan	1849	388,090.75	44,548	24,865
Feb	1849	412,763.5	137,456	40,840.375
Mar	1849	266,543.75	44,837	22,585.25
Apr	1849	451,911.13	132,323	11,638.75
May	1849	258,622.63	48,530	22,759.625
Jun	1849	260,020	33,868	15,295.25
Jul	1849	269,249.25	44,758	17,538.5
Aug	1849	113,563.25	33,755	14,378
Sep	1849	150,495.63	67,946	59,273.75
Oct	1849		15,129	66,108.875
Nov	1849	419,440.25	70,503	
Dec	1849	331,223.63	72,260	14,444.25
Jan	1850	274,557.75	78,905	26,590.875
Feb	1850	263,554	148,634.75	38,426.375
Mar	1850	460,778.13	103,659	31,611.375
Apr	1850	389,354.63	91,144.5	22,677.375
May	1850	339,299.38	111,792	58,480.5
Jun	1850	198,677.25	72,463.625	29,094.25
Jul	1850	294,801.88	79,217	41,486.125
Aug	1850	205,087.5	119,886	20,152
Sep	1850	540,201.5	258,124	58,974
Oct	1850	691,468.13	168,143.25	104,698.13
Nov	1850	695,097.25	117,989	65,851.5
Dec	1850	626,940	67,724.5	89,150.75
Jan	1851	625,476	210,958.5	78,494.5

(continued)

(continued)

Value of securities traded on each exchange (in USD) ($)				
	Year	*NYSE*	*Philadelphia*	*Boston*
Feb	1851	440,195	99,272	68,911.75
Mar	1851	410,294	191,422	57,058.375
Apr	1851	406,447	65,412	88,116.2
May	1851	801,675	128,264	108,566.88
Jun	1851	463,018	71,158.5	52,599.75
Jul	1851	830,057	44,954.625	65,903.625
Aug	1851	667,392	79,592.25	155,303.13
Sep	1851	468,145	73,580	74,038
Oct	1851	365,995	43,455	62,701.25
Nov	1851	461,873	111,358	36,718.125
Dec	1851	433,000	57,212.5	26,977.5
Jan	1852	551,391	184,571	49,538.375
Feb	1852	601,166	206,787.88	72,488.75
Mar	1852	547,442	174,356.25	78,734.625
Apr	1852	971,398	137,197.5	118,684.63
May	1852	507,225	115,267.5	107,517.88
Jun	1852	819,594	102,971.5	88,588.625
Jul	1852	598,058	93,426.5	48,220.5
Aug	1852	518,198	108,109.75	53,907.875
Sep	1852	558,233	158,170.75	46,520.25
Oct	1852	910,760	232,244.63	73,161.25
Nov	1852	886,369	318,476.25	114,131.75
Dec	1852	889,084	151,013	108,043.38
Jan	1853	834,953	249,592.75	73,439.5
Feb	1853	815,233	213,169.63	150,297.63
Mar	1853	715,677	157,621.25	103,419.88
Apr	1853	729,880	221,018.38	109,803.88
May	1853	735,102	137,713.63	65,770.25
Jun	1853	621,969	116,071.13	42,913.375
Jul	1853	662,234	26,275	54,363.5
Aug	1853	722,710	162,605.75	78,707
Sep	1853	888,220	89,862.25	75,787.5
Oct	1853	524,136	43,823.75	49,700.625
Nov	1853	865,641	46,486.5	137,963.88
Dec	1853	894,498	58,570.25	37,580.25
Jan	1854	520,490.5	99,588.375	101,122.75
Feb	1854	922,375.4	150,082.13	46,933.25
Mar	1854	783,920	35,341.25	35,906.5
Apr	1854	529,591	86,782	29,532.25
May	1854	1,098,964	58,779.375	43,181.25

(continued)

(continued)

Value of securities traded on each exchange (in USD) ($)				
	Year	*NYSE*	*Philadelphia*	*Boston*
Jun	1854	997,862	43,900.25	102,781.38
Jul	1854	497,910	48,381.375	11,052.75
Aug	1854	397,918	65,067.25	
Sep	1854	622,979	60,915.5	13,962.75
Oct	1854	479,569	47,939	
Nov	1854	622,800	74,781.375	
Dec	1854	612,959	59,417.75	
Jan	1855	678,301.9	57,486.125	
Feb	1855	675,357	117,056.88	
Mar	1855	759,321.1	59,842.375	
Apr	1855	823,205.8	93,252.5	23,876.625
May	1855	1,112,821	96,437	43,906.125
Jun	1855	1,131,329	82,830.375	22,816.625
Jul	1855	1,206,921	98,431.125	8957.75
Aug	1855	1,496,274	124,172.88	12,626.75
Sep	1855	1,577,634	124,438.13	39,868.875
Oct	1855	1,513,988	76,525.25	101,580
Nov	1855	821,796.8	58,054	17,978.375
Dec	1855	1,260,370	31,431.125	
Jan	1856	705,062.8	91,581.75	
Feb	1856	1,027,448	121,480.88	
Mar	1856	848,679.3	52,946.5	
Apr	1856	1,734,651	52,598.5	
May	1856	1,097,597	104,411.5	
Jun	1856	1,725,944	45,127.5	6211.25
Jul	1856	1,024,233	37,561.25	
Aug	1856	961,936.8	27,619.5	
Sep	1856	1,807,580	55,717.75	6655.125
Oct	1856	2,454,518	70,676.75	132,275.13
Nov	1856	1,969,934	60,271.25	103,844.625
Dec	1856	1,202,490.8	58,273.25	
Jan	1857	1,495,497	42,219.75	
Feb	1857	1,544,047	62,182.875	
Mar	1857	1,495,147.4	116,796.13	19,863.875
Apr	1857	1,372,871.3	79,685.75	16,400.5
May	1857	1,533,383.8	104,727.13	7208.875
Jun	1857	1,708,941.5	72,093.5	
Jul	1857	1,245,958.5		8097.5
Aug	1857	821,538.38		2818.75
Sep	1857	502,672		6481

(continued)

(continued)

Value of securities traded on each exchange (in USD) ($)				
	Year	*NYSE*	*Philadelphia*	*Boston*
Oct	1857	523,757.75		14,985.25
Nov	1857	595,817.5		5767
Dec	1857	595,990.63		13,835
Jan	1858	1,090,855.9		60,329.125
Feb	1858	1,512,525		59,822.625
Mar	1858	941,621.75		6234.875
Apr	1858	925,531.5		33,184.375
May	1858	891,938.25		
Jun	1858	466,003.88		12,928
Jul	1858	684,042		58,359
Aug	1858	778,831.38		10,571.875
Sep	1858	1,183,020.1		25,481
Oct	1858	1,203,016.3		
Nov	1858	920,626.38		
Dec	1858	905,967.5		
Jan	1859	1,475,807.6		26,013.625
Feb	1859	1,451,264.9		
Mar	1859	1,461,110.5		
Apr	1859	1,028,379.6		
May	1859	625,355		
Jun	1859	825,209.38		19,809.5
Jul	1859	405,710		139,959.19
Aug	1859	1,705,792.1		30,305.125
Sep	1859	814,147.63		17,930.25
Oct	1859	887,252.5		6739.25
Nov	1859	1,335,270.6		43,342.25
Dec	1859	650,043.63		69,071.625
Jan	1860	1,293,266.6		35,148
Feb	1860	1,056,399.5		49,237.375
Mar	1860	1,464,031		
Apr	1860	1,254,512.9		
May	1860	1,025,819		
Jun	1860	691,776		
Jul	1860	1,626,479.4		
Aug	1860	1,699,672.3		
Sep	1860	2,259,831.4		
Oct	1860	1,559,985		
Nov	1860	731,783.25		
Dec	1860	681,336.13		45,072
Jan	1861	596,949.5		32,636.25

(continued)

(continued)

Value of securities traded on each exchange (in USD) ($)				
	Year	*NYSE*	*Philadelphia*	*Boston*
Feb	1861	1,721,655.6		30,371.125
Mar	1861	699,290.63		135,921
Apr	1861	629,574.25		18,352.875
May	1861	646,513.63		11,941.875
Jun	1861	572,394		29,704
Jul	1861	416,251.25		
Aug	1861	406,832.25		
Sep	1861	472,651.25		
Oct	1861	955,071		
Nov	1861	743,188.25		
Dec	1861	881,891		
Jan	1862	1,441,188.8		
Feb	1862	1,205,508.8		
Mar	1862	783,650		178,454.13
Apr	1862	2,019,496.8		170,340.88
May	1862	1,034,167.9		324,211.63
Jun	1862	999,574.5		142,463
Jul	1862	1,073,869.3		166,674.88
Aug	1862	1,041,026.1		156,309.5
Sep	1862	3,316,137.1		258,660
Oct	1862	2,476,122.6		379,276
Nov	1862	2,236,807.8		309,397.88
Dec	1862	3,708,067.3		363,988.88
Jan	1863	3,805,337.5		
Feb	1863	4,111,580.5		
Mar	1863	2,737,780.1		
Apr	1863	7,326,733.8		
May	1863	6,356,955.5		
Jun	1863	4,146,739.5		
Jul	1863	5,091,655.3		
Aug	1863	5,230,159.8		
Sep	1863	5,258,341.5		
Oct	1863	7,493,166.5		
Nov	1863	5,487,706.3		
Dec	1863	4,739,938.1		
Jan	1864			
Feb	1864			
Mar	1864			
Apr	1864			
May	1864			

(continued)

(continued)

Value of securities traded on each exchange (in USD) ($)				
	Year	*NYSE*	*Philadelphia*	*Boston*
Jun	1864	3,287,157.8		
Jul	1864	3,752,084.5		
Aug	1864	3,774,670.5		
Sep	1864	6,598,423.8		
Oct	1864	3,184,327.3		
Nov	1864	3,232,762.5		
Dec	1864	3,969,405		
Jan	1865	3,152,980.6		
Feb	1865	3,477,645.5		
Mar	1865	3,604,660		
Apr	1865	2,155,200.3		
May	1865	2,587,040		
Jun	1865	1,752,466.3		
Jul	1865	2,569,057.5		
Aug	1865	1,257,347		
Sep	1865			
Oct	1865			
Nov	1865	1,855,076.5		

Source Contemporary Newspapers as detailed in Table 6.1

Appendix B: Bid Ask Spreads

Average Bid ask spread for each exchange

	Year	*NYSE*	*Philadelphia*	*Boston*
Mar	1830	0.02133273		
Apr	1830	0.02337177		
May	1830	0.01852008		
Jun	1830	0.05153791		
Jul	1830	0.0118913		
Aug	1830	0.01684847		
Sep	1830	0.01966015		
Oct	1830	0.01761295		
Nov	1830	0.02173124		
Dec	1830	0.0272245		
Jan	1831	0.02876939		
Feb	1831	0.02993669		
Mar	1831	0.02246103		
Apr	1831	0.021472		
May	1831	0.01693129		
Jun	1831	0.01871367		
Jul	1831			
Aug	1831	0.0163169		
Sep	1831			
Oct	1831	0.01732136		
Nov	1831	0.02106144		
Dec	1831			
Jan	1832			

(continued)

S. Garg, *The Telegraph and Stock Exchanges*, Palgrave Studies in Economic History, https://doi.org/10.1007/978-3-031-40407-8

(continued)

Average Bid ask spread for each exchange				
	Year	*NYSE*	*Philadelphia*	*Boston*
Feb	1832	0.0221066		
Mar	1832			
Apr	1832			
May	1832	0.02149421		
Jun	1832	0.02554883		
Jul	1832		0.05010181	
Aug	1832	0.02579044	0.05963818	
Sep	1832	0.02364416	0.05664612	
Oct	1832	0.02321173	0.0569551	
Nov	1832	0.02262325	0.07458252	
Dec	1832	0.02105157	0.07122824	
Jan	1833		0.05627733	
Feb	1833		0.07456492	
Mar	1833		0.07129385	
Apr	1833		0.06738035	
May	1833		0.0712929	
Jun	1833		0.08401419	
Jul	1833		0.07730606	
Aug	1833		0.06823557	
Sep	1833		0.06032133	
Oct	1833		0.06057731	
Nov	1833		0.07826504	
Dec	1833		0.1102457	
Jan	1834	0.02558513	0.09712813	
Feb	1834	0.03191057	0.09911352	
Mar	1834	0.02102043	0.09016914	
Apr	1834	0.01961167	0.09010729	
May	1834	0.01991554	0.06914282	
Jun	1834	0.01791491	0.10236237	
Jul	1834	0.01830153	0.12454306	
Aug	1834		0.11259064	
Sep	1834	0.01644588	0.09795943	
Oct	1834		0.06835116	
Nov	1834		0.08090337	
Dec	1834		0.08559591	
Jan	1835		0.1059968	
Feb	1835	0.02481039	0.08936848	
Mar	1835	0.01529765	0.07743999	
Apr	1835	0.01334598	0.04380417	
May	1835	0.03195385	0.05859463	

(continued)

(continued)

Average Bid ask spread for each exchange				
	Year	*NYSE*	*Philadelphia*	*Boston*
Jun	1835		0.05759506	
Jul	1835		0.07156895	0.01834681
Aug	1835		0.11520029	0.01769093
Sep	1835		0.10078926	0.01562728
Oct	1835		0.06816162	0.01869351
Nov	1835		0.09522155	0.01977892
Dec	1835		0.08257912	0.02054834
Jan	1836			0.02146973
Feb	1836			0.0193383
Mar	1836			0.01845148
Apr	1836			0.01775517
May	1836	0.03182408		0.02314882
Jun	1836	0.03199936		0.01954125
Jul	1836	0.0309302		0.0170882
Aug	1836	0.07623553		0.01537986
Sep	1836	0.04602141		0.01503613
Oct	1836	0.02915178		
Nov	1836	0.0272871		
Dec	1836	0.0241879		
Jan	1837	0.02842941		
Feb	1837	0.03462937		
Mar	1837	0.04419295		
Apr	1837	0.0753054		
May	1837	0.06166145		
Jun	1837	0.05944627		
Jul	1837	0.04848783		
Aug	1837	0.04908751		
Sep	1837	0.04259823		
Oct	1837	0.05319118		
Nov	1837	0.04228796		
Dec	1837	0.04969344		
Jan	1838	0.05391262	0.13062515	
Feb	1838	0.05562666	0.1084898	
Mar	1838	0.05044746	0.12087231	
Apr	1838	0.04362113	0.10872655	
May	1838	0.04070933	0.10028403	
Jun	1838	0.03466067	0.09938339	
Jul	1838	0.02722376	0.09921441	
Aug	1838	0.0324567	0.09681461	
Sep	1838	0.03496746	0.0879767	

(continued)

(continued)

Average Bid ask spread for each exchange

	Year	*NYSE*	*Philadelphia*	*Boston*
Oct	1838	0.04835485	0.07510583	
Nov	1838	0.05814446	0.08410171	
Dec	1838	0.03164847		
Jan	1839	0.036155		
Feb	1839	0.04228751		
Mar	1839	0.0387066		
Apr	1839	0.04125482	0.12544012	
May	1839	0.02570353	0.12645408	
Jun	1839	0.03768256	0.15209135	
Jul	1839	0.03272068	0.13605427	
Aug	1839	0.04154096	0.14231213	
Sep	1839	0.05716172	0.11644361	
Oct	1839	0.06059584	0.10914624	
Nov	1839	0.05458772	0.11746622	
Dec	1839	0.07676488	0.14217487	
Jan	1840	0.09743865	0.1146245	
Feb	1840	0.1274597	0.13812835	
Mar	1840	0.08093005	0.16713676	
Apr	1840	0.0761048	0.12510323	
May	1840	0.07091063	0.1161988	
Jun	1840	0.09942097	0.10130832	
Jul	1840	0.12316305	0.13470675	
Aug	1840	0.06195689	0.07792996	
Sep	1840	0.06154335	0.11626014	
Oct	1840	0.06374645	0.15868513	
Nov	1840	0.05390947	0.08445311	
Dec	1840	0.06743433	0.07349405	
Jan	1841	0.06849832	0.10884721	
Feb	1841	0.0329812	0.08322741	
Mar	1841	0.05775054	0.10477596	
Apr	1841	0.07832196	0.09663552	
May	1841	0.06524898	0.17454038	
Jun	1841	0.06211738	0.18452058	
Jul	1841		0.17812838	
Aug	1841		0.13131343	
Sep	1841	0.08160007	0.14048702	
Oct	1841	0.09611368	0.11477216	
Nov	1841	0.11900363	0.1198542	
Dec	1841	0.125664	0.13844159	
Jan	1842	0.17431746	0.20062062	

(continued)

(continued)

Average Bid ask spread for each exchange

	Year	*NYSE*	*Philadelphia*	*Boston*
Feb	1842	0.16356272	0.19367408	
Mar	1842	0.16892914	0.11849686	
Apr	1842	0.211883	0.1795556	
May	1842	0.13521096	0.2015995	
Jun	1842	0.11180946	0.12418663	
Jul	1842	0.19353244	0.3132917	
Aug	1842		0.35423566	
Sep	1842		0.29851647	
Oct	1842		0.33121258	
Nov	1842		0.28594245	
Dec	1842		0.32882828	
Jan	1843	0.0599587	0.33646332	
Feb	1843	0.0573809	0.28545733	
Mar	1843	0.05305483	0.27775952	
Apr	1843	0.02061688	0.40798926	
May	1843	0.02783935	0.11082281	
Jun	1843	0.05552209	0.19757087	
Jul	1843	0.04134399	0.14499788	
Aug	1843	0.05124367	0.1403911	
Sep	1843		0.07114344	
Oct	1843		0.14334191	
Nov	1843		0.13657514	
Dec	1843		0.13140125	
Jan	1844	0.03109068	0.06434731	
Feb	1844	0.0176936	0.09352609	
Mar	1844	0.02879551	0.04896441	
Apr	1844	0.01903875	0.0645665	
May	1844		0.06044301	
Jun	1844		0.08056211	
Jul	1844		0.06207363	
Aug	1844		0.04991248	0.02710881
Sep	1844		0.0782938	0.01898623
Oct	1844		0.04555465	0.01939252
Nov	1844		0.05967615	0.0262826
Dec	1844	0.07491207	0.11373386	0.02094892
Jan	1845		0.03650124	0.02074333
Feb	1845		0.04691024	
Mar	1845	0.01869786	0.04610471	
Apr	1845		0.04591336	0.02010814
May	1845		0.04068999	0.02196161

(continued)

(continued)

Average Bid ask spread for each exchange				
	Year	*NYSE*	*Philadelphia*	*Boston*
Jun	1845		0.03715384	0.01539874
Jul	1845	0.07470142	0.05114263	0.02077943
Aug	1845	0.03558687	0.06570271	0.02113698
Sep	1845	0.0310932	0.0618604	0.0180897
Oct	1845	0.0383487	0.0587737	0.0185972
Nov	1845	0.0235138	0.0509847	0.0320374
Dec	1845		0.1004548	0.0415948
Jan	1846			0.0415715
Feb	1846			0.0359408
Mar	1846	0.0328271		0.0392467
Apr	1846			0.0604538
May	1846			0.0481816
Jun	1846	0.0161776	0.0417906	0.0339494
Jul	1846		0.1150315	0.0436483
Aug	1846		0.0407307	0.0309829
Sep	1846		0.1059961	0.0371579
Oct	1846		0.0773656	0.0530017
Nov	1846		0.0717183	0.0671888
Dec	1846		0.0780010	0.0746120
Jan	1847		0.0712773	0.0530878
Feb	1847		0.0853357	0.0427213
Mar	1847		0.0758291	0.0352720
Apr	1847		0.0803667	0.0362860
May	1847		0.0709805	0.0368414
Jun	1847		0.0526942	0.0580076
Jul	1847		0.0439790	0.0246196
Aug	1847		0.0807172	0.0255198
Sep	1847	0.0321212	0.0659887	0.0345642
Oct	1847	0.0340070	0.1008201	0.0320097
Nov	1847		0.0538822	0.0535751
Dec	1847		0.0476931	0.0380295
Jan	1848	0.0311503	0.0437625	0.0362541
Feb	1848		0.0412957	0.0575759
Mar	1848	0.0301633	0.0383667	0.0409660
Apr	1848		0.0403607	0.0478041
May	1848		0.0474127	0.0449820
Jun	1848		0.0540371	0.0557378
Jul	1848		0.0541836	0.0571643
Aug	1848		0.0427852	0.0565038
Sep	1848		0.0371499	0.0588602

(continued)

(continued)

Average Bid ask spread for each exchange

	Year	*NYSE*	*Philadelphia*	*Boston*
Oct	1848		0.0395379	0.0673859
Nov	1848	0.0695479	0.0275464	0.0644327
Dec	1848	0.0311696	0.0357697	0.0705346
Jan	1849		0.0822116	0.0482283
Feb	1849	0.0257058	0.0270330	0.0601720
Mar	1849	0.0198901	0.0322386	0.0519590
Apr	1849	0.0398550	0.0329309	0.0525930
May	1849	0.0201139	0.0288963	0.0546451
Jun	1849	0.0430583	0.0277556	0.0413543
Jul	1849	0.0531040	0.0335581	0.0282270
Aug	1849	0.0223162	0.0235987	0.0297893
Sep	1849	0.0300858	0.0259350	0.0329081
Oct	1849	0.0426433	0.0511889	0.0324966
Nov	1849	0.0438738	0.0601981	0.0311175
Dec	1849	0.0148775	0.0499698	0.0269244
Jan	1850	0.0253071	0.0544236	0.0352004
Feb	1850	0.0254480	0.1130949	0.0361186
Mar	1850	0.0257528	0.1223490	0.0316481
Apr	1850	0.0108454	0.0903716	0.0425656
May	1850	0.0191488	0.1151131	0.0364239
Jun	1850	0.0113831	0.0887195	0.0521859
Jul	1850	0.0167803	0.0218102	0.0381883
Aug	1850	0.0101207	0.0292254	0.0343390
Sep	1850	0.0149576	0.0301980	0.0427941
Oct	1850	0.0214690	0.0304913	0.0491558
Nov	1850	0.0160736	0.0250840	0.0545158
Dec	1850	0.0203447	0.0175661	0.0476314
Jan	1851	0.0196115	0.0247284	0.0436791
Feb	1851	0.0337513	0.0183395	0.0715422
Mar	1851	0.0228599	0.0171612	0.0535849
Apr	1851	0.0046889	0.0130360	0.0575613
May	1851	0.0150059	0.0135622	0.0633220
Jun	1851	0.0385230	0.0167475	0.0408862
Jul	1851	0.0170904	0.0189822	0.0433258
Aug	1851	0.0382305	0.0196727	0.0407111
Sep	1851	0.0323181	0.0262032	0.0489829
Oct	1851	0.0247273	0.0585558	0.0532161
Nov	1851	0.0258721	0.0328076	0.0438991
Dec	1851		0.0226851	0.0513828
Jan	1852	0.0165140	0.0293601	

(continued)

(continued)

Average Bid ask spread for each exchange

	Year	*NYSE*	*Philadelphia*	*Boston*
Feb	1852		0.0299892	
Mar	1852	0.0198139	0.0273492	
Apr	1852	0.0167959	0.0280657	
May	1852	0.0085527	0.0091049	
Jun	1852		0.0175109	
Jul	1852		0.0218835	
Aug	1852		0.0280385	
Sep	1852	0.0139449	0.0232730	
Oct	1852		0.0290890	
Nov	1852		0.0281574	
Dec	1852		0.0297908	
Jan	1853		0.0327275	
Feb	1853		0.0292323	
Mar	1853		0.0262207	
Apr	1853		0.0258837	
May	1853		0.0360273	
Jun	1853		0.0373701	
Jul	1853		0.02779818	
Aug	1853		0.03108742	
Sep	1853		0.0179816	
Oct	1853		0.01580375	
Nov	1853		0.01799273	
Dec	1853		0.0167961	
Jan	1854		0.01815107	
Feb	1854		0.01872238	
Mar	1854		0.01828247	
Apr	1854		0.01641653	
May	1854		0.00927655	
Jun	1854		0.02121977	
Jul	1854		0.02909833	
Aug	1854		0.04426584	
Sep	1854		0.04180398	
Oct	1854		0.03305634	
Nov	1854		0.04152945	
Dec	1854		0.02891674	
Jan	1855		0.03276432	
Feb	1855		0.02553887	
Mar	1855		0.02531659	
Apr	1855		0.02482114	
May	1855		0.01763424	

(continued)

(continued)

Average Bid ask spread for each exchange

	Year	*NYSE*	*Philadelphia*	*Boston*
Jun	1855		0.02691716	
Jul	1855		0.02902178	
Aug	1855		0.02850795	
Sep	1855		0.03442305	
Oct	1855		0.03114417	
Nov	1855		0.03003521	
Dec	1855		0.05552557	
Jan	1856		0.02292243	
Feb	1856		0.02516471	
Mar	1856		0.02758109	
Apr	1856		0.02718993	
May	1856		0.02725457	
Jun	1856		0.02196495	
Jul	1856		0.02764325	
Aug	1856		0.02467117	
Sep	1856		0.02368977	
Oct	1856		0.02179909	
Nov	1856		0.04615255	
Dec	1856		0.04539076	
Jan	1857		0.03342983	
Feb	1857		0.0648546	
Mar	1857		0.0177013	0.06114885
Apr	1857		0.01960519	0.04015467
May	1857		0.03432957	0.05583614
Jun	1857		0.03353342	
Jul	1857		0.04239722	0.09903762
Aug	1857		0.02838085	0.06413446
Sep	1857		0.13496815	0.14383631
Oct	1857		0.11294266	0.18679002
Nov	1857		0.10523813	
Dec	1857		0.14112549	
Jan	1858		0.08951826	
Feb	1858		0.1034508	
Mar	1858		0.10329365	
Apr	1858		0.06381478	
May	1858		0.09858903	
Jun	1858		0.08006635	
Jul	1858		0.10058776	0.04644432
Aug	1858		0.07834711	0.09775731
Sep	1858		0.06127693	0.19765372

(continued)

(continued)

Average Bid ask spread for each exchange

	Year	*NYSE*	*Philadelphia*	*Boston*
Oct	1858		0.04195785	
Nov	1858		0.02731505	
Dec	1858			
Jan	1859			
Feb	1859		0.04350047	
Mar	1859		0.04462843	
Apr	1859			
May	1859		0.03827404	
Jun	1859		0.06286711	
Jul	1859		0.09293753	
Aug	1859			
Sep	1859			
Oct	1859			
Nov	1859			
Dec	1859			
Jan	1860			
Feb	1860			
Mar	1860			
Apr	1860			
May	1860			
Jun	1860			
Jul	1860			
Aug	1860			
Sep	1860		0.02140863	
Oct	1860		0.07020773	
Nov	1860		0.09808723	
Dec	1860		0.1589516	
Jan	1861			0.04578878
Feb	1861			0.06121737
Mar	1861			0.05821802
Apr	1861			0.15060841
May	1861			0.15920264
Jun	1861			
Jul	1861			
Aug	1861			
Sep	1861			
Oct	1861			
Nov	1861			
Dec	1861			
Jan	1862			

(continued)

(continued)

Average Bid ask spread for each exchange				
	Year	*NYSE*	*Philadelphia*	*Boston*
Feb	1862			
Mar	1862			0.02252174
Apr	1862			0.02200108
May	1862			0.01325514
Jun	1862			0.01943125
Jul	1862			0.01432227
Aug	1862			0.01718841
Sep	1862			0.02170979
Oct	1862			0.01959748
Nov	1862			0.01595166
Dec	1862			0.0166941

Source Contemporary Newspapers as detailed in Table 6.1

Appendix C: Charges for Telegraph Dispatches from New York City as Reported in 1852

Table 8.7: Cost for transmission in cents (1/100 USD)

City	*State/country*	*Ten words*	*Each additional word*
Adrian	Mich.	95	5
Akron	Ohio	65	4
Albany	N.Y.	30	2
Albion	N.Y.	40	3
Albion	Mich.	90	5
Alleghany City	Pa.	60	4
Alexandria	Va.	56	5
Algonac	Mich.	110	6
Allentown	Pa.	40	4
Alton	Ill.	150	9
Amherst	Me.	153	9
Ann Arbor	Mich.	90	5
Appleton	Wis.	180	10
Ashland	Ohio	75	5
Ashtabula	Ohio	50	3
Athens	Ohio	100	7
Athens	Ga.	95	9
Atlanta	Ga.	191	12
Attica	Ind.	110	6
Auburn	N.Y.	40	3
Augusta	Me.	65	4
Augusta	Ga.	133	9

(continued)

S. Garg, *The Telegraph and Stock Exchanges*, Palgrave Studies in Economic History, https://doi.org/10.1007/978-3-031-40407-8

(continued)

Table 8.7: Cost for transmission in cents (1/100 USD)

City	*State/country*	*Ten words*	*Each additional word*
Aurora	Ill.	130	7
Avon Springs	N.Y.	45	3
Baltimore	Md.	50	4
Bangor	Me.	80	4
Baraboo	Wis.	200	11
Bardstown	Ky.	130	9
Batavia	N.Y.	40	3
Batavia	Ill.	125	7
Bath	Me.	70	4
Baton Rouge	La.	235	16
Battle Creek	Mich.	90	5
Beardstown	Ill.	140	8
Beaver	Pa.	70	4
Beaver Meadow	Pa.	50	4
Bedford	Pa.	50	3
Belfast	Me.	65	4
Bellefontaine	Ohio	80	6
Belleville	Can.	75	6
Belvidere	Ill.	130	8
Bellville	Ohio	75	4
Beloit	Wis.	150	9
Bennington	Vt.	55	4
Berthier	Can.	110	9
Bethlehem	Pa.	40	4
Binghamton	N.Y.	40	3
Bloomington	Iowa	150	9
Bolivar	Ohio	75	4
Boston	Mass.	20	2
Bowmansville	Can.	75	6
Brantford	Can.	83	6
Brattleboro	Vt.	45	4
Bridgeport	Conn.	20	2
Bristol	Mich.	105	6
Brockport	N.Y.	40	3
Brockville	Can.	90	7
Brownsville	Pa.	50	4
Buffalo	N.Y.	40	4
Burlington	Vt.	60	4
Burlington	Iowa	135	10
Cadiz	Ohio	80	4

(continued)

(continued)

Table 8.7: Cost for transmission in cents (1/100 USD)

City	*State/country*	*Ten words*	*Each additional word*
Cahawba	Ala.	190	12
Cairo	Ill.	150	9
Calais	Me.	90	5
Cambridge City	Ind.	110	6
Camden	S.C.	103	7
Canal Dover	Ohio	100	7
Canandaigua	N.Y.	40	3
Canton	Miss.	175	11
Cantwell's Bridge	Del.	45	4
Carbondale	Pa.	40	3
Carlisle	Pa.	40	3
Carlisle	Ind.	110	6
Carmel	N.Y.	20	1
Castleton	Vt.	55	4
Catskill	N.Y.	20	1
Catasauqua	Pa.	40	4
Cedarburg	Wis.	150	8
Chagrin Falls	Ohio	75	4
Chambersburg	Pa.	40	3
Charleston	S.C.	119	8
Cheraw	S.C.	97	7
Cherryfield	Me.	90	5
Chicago	Ill.	100	6
Chillicothe	Ohio	100	7
Chippewa	Can.	63	6
Cincinnati	Ohio	75	5
Circleville	Ohio	100	6
Clarksville	Tenn.	125	9
Clarkston	Mich.	100	6
Claremont	N.H.	45	4
Cleveland	Ohio	50	3
Clinton	La.	200	14
Coburg	Can.	50	4
Cold Spring	N.Y.	20	1
Coldwater	Mich.	100	5
Columbia	Pa.	55	5
Columbia	S.C.	106	7
Columbia	Tenn.	140	9
Columbus	Ohio	80	5
Columbus	Ga.	175	11

(continued)

(continued)

Table 8.7: Cost for transmission in cents (1/100 USD)

City	*State/country*	*Ten words*	*Each additional word*
Columbus	Miss.	175	12
Columbus	Tenn.	175	11
Concord	N.H.	45	4
Conneaut	Ohio	50	3
Connellsville	Ind.	105	7
Constantine	Mich.	105	6
Cooperstown	N.Y.	40	3
Corning	N.Y.	45	3
Cornwall	Can.	85	7
Covington	Ind.	110	6
Coxsackie	N.Y.	20	1
Crown Point	Mich.	110	6
Cumberland	Md.	80	7
Cuyahoga Falls	Ohio	65	4
Cuylerville	N.Y.	45	3
Damariscotta	Me.	60	4
Dansville	N.Y.	45	3
Dansville	Ill.	100	6
Darling	Can.	75	6
Dayton	Ohio	100	6
Dubuque	Ill.	140	6
Defiance	Ohio	95	6
Delaware	Pa.	25	2
Delaware City	Del.	40	4
Delphi	Ind.	100	6
Deposit	Pa.	40	2
Detroit	Mich.	75	4
Dixon	Ill.	135	8
Dodgeville	Wis.	160	10
Dover	Del.	50	5
Dover	Ohio	75	4
Doylestown	Pa.	45	4
Dresden	Ohio	75	4
Dundas	Can.	83	6
Dundee	Ill.	135	7
Dunkirk	N.Y.	50	3
Easton	Pa.	40	4
Eastport	Me.	90	5
East Machias	Me.	90	5
Eaton	Ohio	95	6

(continued)

(continued)

Table 8.7: Cost for transmission in cents (1/100 USD)

City	*State/country*	*Ten words*	*Each additional word*
Eddyville	Ky.	135	8
Elgin	Ill.	130	7
Elkhart	Mich.	105	6
Ellsworth	Me.	70	4
Elmira	N.Y.	40	2
Elyria	Ohio	60	4
Enfield	N.H.	50	4
Erie	Pa.	50	3
Eugene	Ind.	110	6
Evansville	Ind.	160	11
Fairport	Ohio	55	4
Fall River	Mass.	20	2
Fayetteville	N.C.	90	7
Flint	Mich.	105	6
Fond Du Lac	Wis.	170	10
Frankfort	Ky.	140	9
Franklin	N.H.	45	4
Franklin Mills	Ohio	75	4
Fredericksburg	Va.	61	5
Frederick City	Md.	75	7
Fredericktown	N.B.	128	7
Fredonia	N.Y.	50	3
Freemont	Ohio	60	4
Freeport	Ill.	140	9
Fort Atkinson	Wis.	150	9
Fort Plain	N.Y.	30	2
Fort Wayne	Ind.	100	6
Fort Winnebago	Wis.	200	11
Fulton	N.Y.	40	3
Fulton	Ohio	75	4
Galatin	Miss.	190	13
Galena	Ill.	140	8
Gallipolis	Ohio	115	8
Gardiner	Me.	65	4
Geneva	N.Y.	40	3
Geneva	Ill.	135	7
Geneseo	N.Y.	45	3
Georgetown	D.C.	55	5
Germantown	Pa.	45	4
Girard	Pa.	50	3

(continued)

(continued)

Table 8.7: Cost for transmission in cents (1/100 USD)

City	*State/country*	*Ten words*	*Each additional word*
Glasgow	Ky.	140	9
Goodrich	Mich.	105	6
Goshen	N.Y.	25	1
Goshen	Ind.	105	6
Granville	Ohio	80	5
Green Bay	Wis.	200	11
Greenbush	Wis.	160	10
Greencastle	Ind.	110	6
Greenfield	Mass.	45	4
Greensburg	Pa.	60	4
Griffin	Ga.	186	12
Halifax	N.S.	165	10
Hallowell	Me.	65	4
Hamilton	Ohio	110	6
Hamilton	Can.	63	5
Hannibal	Mo.	150	9
Hards	N.B.	165	10
Harper's Ferry	Va.	75	7
Harrisburg	Pa.	45	4
Hartford	Conn.	20	2
Havre De Grace	Md.	45	3
Hazel Green	Wis.	160	9
Hebron	Ohio	80	5
Herkimer	N.Y.	30	2
Hillsboro	Ill.	130	8
Hollidaysburg	Pa.	60	4
Holly Springs	Ala.	190	13
Honesdale	Pa.	25	2
Hudson	N.Y.	20	2
Hudson	Ohio	65	4
Hudson	Mich.	95	5
Huntington	Ind.	95	6
Indianapolis	Ind.	110	6
Iowa City	Iowa	175	11
Ithaca	N.Y.	65	4
Jacinto	Miss.	155	11
Jackson	Miss.	220	11
Jackson	Mich.	90	5
Jacksonville	Ill.	145	9
Janesville	Wis.	140	9

(continued)

(continued)

Table 8.7: Cost for transmission in cents (1/100 USD)

City	*State/country*	*Ten words*	*Each additional word*
Jefferson	N.Y.	65	4
Jefferson	Miss.	150	8
Jefferson	Wis.	150	9
Jeffersonville	Ind.	110	8
Jersey City	N.J.	20	2
Jonesville	Mich.	95	5
Juliet	Ill.	130	8
Junction	Ohio	90	6
Junction	Vt.	50	2
Kalamazoo	Mich.	90	5
Kenosha	Wis.	130	7
Kenton	Ohio	80	6
Keokuk	Iowa	150	9
Kingston	N.Y.	20	1
Kingston	Can.	75	6
Lafayette	Ind.	100	6
Lake Mills	Ohio	150	9
Lancaster	Pa.	45	4
Lancaster	Ill.	155	10
Lancaster	Ohio	95	6
Lancaster	Wis.	165	10
La Porte	Ind.	100	6
LaSalle	Ill.	140	8
Lawrenceburg	Ind.	95	6
Lebanon	N.H.	50	4
Lewiston	N.Y.	50	4
Lexington	Ky.	120	8
Liberty	Miss.	195	12
Lima	Ind.	100	6
Little Falls	N.Y.	30	2
Little Fort	Ill.	130	8
Lockport	N.Y.	40	3
Lockport	Ill.	130	8
Logansport	Ind.	100	6
London	Can.	88	7
Louisville	Ky.	120	8
Lowell	Mass.	45	4
Lowell	Ohio	80	4
Lower Sandusky	Ohio	70	4
Macon	Ga.	166	10

(continued)

(continued)

Table 8.7: Cost for transmission in cents (1/100 USD)

City	*State/country*	*Ten words*	*Each additional word*
Madison	Ind.	120	7
Madison	Wis.	150	9
Manchester	Vt.	55	4
Manchester	N.H.	55	4
Mansfield	Ohio	75	4
Marengo	Ill.	130	8
Marietta	Ohio	110	7
Marshall	Mich.	90	5
Martinsburg	Va.	75	6
Massillon	Ohio	65	4
Maumee City	Ohio	70	4
Maysville	Kt.	100	6
Meadville	Pa.	70	5
Medina	N.Y.	40	3
Medina	Ohio	75	4
Memphis	Tenn.	175	13
Menasha	Wis.	190	10
Meriden	Conn.	20	2
Michigan City	Ind.	100	5
Middlebury	Vt.	60	4
Middleton	Ohio	110	6
Middletown	Conn.	20	2
Milan	Ohio	60	4
Milford	Del.	50	5
Milford	Ohio	100	6
Milwaukie	Wis.	130	7
Mineral Point	Wis.	150	9
Milwaukie	Mich.	110	6
Mobile	Ala.	207	12
Monroe	Mich.	70	4
Montezuma	Ind.	120	6
Montgomery	Ala.	185	11
Montpelier	Vt.	85	6
Montreal	Can.	85	7
Montrose	Pa.	40	3
Morris	Ill.	125	7
Morrow	Ohio	90	6
Mt. Carbon	Pa.	50	4
Mt. Clements	Mich.	100	6
Mt. Morris	N.Y.	45	3

(continued)

(continued)

Table 8.7: Cost for transmission in cents (1/100 USD)

City	*State/country*	*Ten words*	*Each additional word*
Mt. Pleasant	Ohio	130	10
Mt. Sterling	Ill.	140	8
Mt. Vernon	Ohio	80	5
Muscatine	Iowa	155	10
Naperville	Ill.	130	7
Nashville	Tenn.	135	10
Nashua	N.H.	45	4
Natchez	Miss.	225	15
Navarre	Ohio	75	4
Neenah	Wis.	190	10
Nazareth	Pa.	45	4
Newark	N.J.	20	2
Newark	Ohio	80	5
New Albany	Ind.	130	8
New Bedford	Mass.	20	2
New Brunswick	N.J.	20	2
New Buffalo	Mich.	100	6
Newburg	N.Y.	20	1
New Castle	Del.	40	4
Newcomerstown	Ohio	70	4
New Haven	Conn.	20	2
New Lisbon	Ohio	70	4
New London	Conn.	20	2
New Orleans	La.	240	14
New Philadelphia	Ohio	80	4
New Richmond	Ohio	105	8
Newport	R.I.	20	2
Newton Falls	Ohio	75	4
New Washington	Ohio	80	6
Niagara	Can.	63	5
Niagara Falls		45	4
Niles	Mich.	95	5
Norfolk	Va.	119	9
Norristown	Pa.	40	4
North Adams	Mass.	40	3
Northampton	Mass.	45	4
Northfield	Vt.	60	5
Norwalk	Conn.	20	2
Nunda	N.Y.	45	3
Ogdensburg	N.Y.	50	3

(continued)

(continued)

Table 8.7: Cost for transmission in cents (1/100 USD)

City	*State/country*	*Ten words*	*Each additional word*
Orwell	Vt.	60	4
Oshawa	Can.	75	6
Oshkosh	Wis.	150	9
Oswego	N.Y.	40	3
Ottawa	Ill.	130	8
Owego	N.Y.	40	3
Ozaukee	Wis.	140	8
Paducah	Ky.	157	9
Painesville	Ohio	50	3
Palmyra	N.Y.	40	3
Palmyra	Wis.	150	10
Paoli	Ind.	140	9
Paris	Ky.	135	9
Paris	Ill.	140	8
Pawtucket	R.I.	20	2
Peekskill	N.Y.	20	1
Penn Yan	N.Y.	60	4
Peoria	Ind.	105	6
Peoria	Ill.	135	8
Perrysville	Ohio	110	6
Peru	Ind.	100	6
Peru	Ill.	130	8
Petersburg	Va.	69	5
Petitcodiac	N.B.	140	8
Phoenixville	Pa.	40	4
Philadelphia	Pa.	25	2
Pictou	N.B.	165	11
Piermont	N.Y.	20	1
Piqua	Ohio	130	8
Piketon	Ohio	125	8
Pikeville	Ala.	165	11
Pittsburg	Pa.	60	4
Pittsfield	Mass.	50	4
Platteville	Wis.	155	10
Pomeroy	Ohio	120	8
Pontiac	Mich.	125	8
Port Clinton	Pa.	50	4
Port Hope	Can.	75	6
Port Huron	Mich.	130	8
Port Jervis	Pa.	25	2

(continued)

(continued)

Table 8.7: Cost for transmission in cents (1/100 USD)

City	*State/country*	*Ten words*	*Each additional word*
Portland	Me.	40	3
Port Richmond	Pa.	40	3
Portsmouth	Ohio	100	7
Portsmouth	N.H.	40	3
Port Washington	Ohio	80	4
Potosi	Mo.	155	10
Pottstown	Pa.	40	4
Pottsville	Pa.	50	4
Poughkeepsie	N.Y.	20	1
Prescott	Can.	85	7
Princeton	N.J.	20	2
Providence	R.I.	20	2
Quebec	Can.	110	9
Queenston	Can.	50	4
Quincy	Ill.	130	8
Racine	Wis.	130	8
Raleigh	N.C.	84	6
Randolph	Vt.	50	4
Ravenna	Ohio	75	4
Reading	Pa.	40	4
Red Hook	N.Y.	20	1
Republic	Ohio	80	6
Richmond	Pa.	35	3
Richmond	Va.	67	5
Richmond	Ind.	110	6
Ripley	Ohio	105	6
Rochester	N. Y.	40	3
Rockford	Ill.	135	7
Rock Island	Ill.	155	10
Rockland	Me.	65	4
Rockton	N.Y.	30	2
Rockton	Ill.	135	7
Rome	N.Y.	30	2
Rondout	N.Y.	20	1
Roscoe	Ohio	80	4
Rushville	Ill.	125	8
Rutland	Vt.	55	4
Sackville	N.B.	140	8
Saginaw	Mich.	140	8
Saco	Me.	40	3

(continued)

(continued)

Table 8.7: Cost for transmission in cents (1/100 USD)

City	*State/country*	*Ten words*	*Each additional word*
Salem	Ill.	150	9
Salem	Ind.	100	6
Sandusky	Ohio	60	4
Saratoga	N.Y.	55	4
Saugerties	N.Y.	20	1
Sauk Prairie	Wis.	210	11
Savannah	Ga.	146	9
Schaghticoke	N.Y.	40	3
Schenectady	N.Y.	30	2
Section Ten	Ohio	100	6
Sheboygan	Wis.	150	9
Sheboygan Falls	Wis.	150	9
Shelbyville	Ohio	105	7
Shelbyville	Ill.	105	7
Shelbyville	Ind.	110	6
Shelbyville	Ky.	120	8
Shullsburg	Wis.	160	10
Sidney	Ohio	100	6
South Bend	Ind.	95	5
Southport	Wis.	130	8
Springfield	Mass.	20	2
Springfield	Vt.	45	4
Springfield	Ohio	80	5
Springfield	Ill.	125	8
Spring Valley	Ohio	90	6
Stamford	Conn.	20	2
Steubenville	Ohio	80	6
St. Albans	Vt.	60	4
St. Catharines	Can.	50	4
St. Charles	Ohio	90	6
St. Clair	Mich.	135	8
St. Genevieve	Mo.	175	10
St. Georges	N.B.	115	6
St. Johns	Can.	100	6
St. Johns	N.B.	115	6
St. Louis	Mo.	145	10
St. Marys	Ohio	100	5
Sturges Prairie	Mich.	100	6
Suffolk	Va.	119	9
Susquehanna	Pa.	40	2

(continued)

(continued)

Table 8.7: Cost for transmission in cents (1/100 USD)

City	*State/country*	*Ten words*	*Each additional word*
Syracuse	N.Y.	40	3
Taunton	Mass.	20	2
Tecumseh	Mich.	90	5
Terre Haute	Ind.	110	6
Theresa	N.Y.	40	3
Thomaston	Me.	65	4
Thompsonville	Conn.	20	2
Three Rivers	Can.	110	9
Tiffin	Ohio	80	6
Toledo	Ohio	70	5
Tonawanda	N.Y.	50	4
Toronto	Can.	63	5
Trenton	N. J.	20	2
Troy	N.Y.	30	2
Troy	Ohio	80	6
Truro	N.B.	165	10
Tuscumbia	Ala.	160	12
Tuscumbia	Mo.	145	10
Uniontown	Pa.	75	5
Urbana	Ohio	80	6
Uhrichsville	Ohio	80	6
Utica	N.Y.	30	2
Valatie	N.Y.	20	1
Valparaiso	Ind.	110	6
Vergennes	Vt.	60	4
Versailles	Ky.	110	7
Vicksburg	Miss.	210	15
Vincennes	Ind.	110	6
Wabash	Ind.	100	6
Waldoboro	Me.	65	4
Warren	R.I.	20	2
Warren	Ohio	75	4
Washington	D.C.	50	5
Washington	Ohio	90	6
Washington	Pa.	85	6
Waterbury	Vt.	60	5
Watertown	N.Y.	50	3
Waukesha	Wis.	125	7
Waynesville	Ohio	90	6
Wellsville	Ohio	70	4

(continued)

(continued)

Table 8.7: Cost for transmission in cents (1/100 USD)

City	*State/country*	*Ten words*	*Each additional word*
Westfield	N.Y.	50	3
West Liberty	Ohio	80	6
West Randolph	Vt.	50	4
West Union	Ohio	105	8
Wheeling	Va.	80	5
Whitby	Can.	75	6
Whitehall	N.Y.	55	4
Whitehaven	Pa.	55	5
White River Junction	Vt.	90	6
Whitewater	Wis.	130	7
Wilkes-Barre	Penn.	55	5
Williamston	Mass.	40	3
Wilmington	Del.	45	4
Winchester	Va.	78	7
Windsor	Vt.	50	4
Woodfield	Ohio	130	9
Woodstock	Vt.	50	5
Woodstock	Can.	88	7
Woodstock	Ill.	130	7
Woonsocket	R.I.	20	2
Worcester	Mass.	20	2
Wooster	Ohio	75	5
Xenia	Ohio	90	6
York	Pa.	50	3
Youngstown	Pa.	80	5
Ypsilanti	Mich.	90	5
Zanesville	Ohio	75	5

Source Jones, Alexander "Historical Sketch of the Electric Telegraph: Including its Rise and Progress in the United States." George P. Putnam, 10 Park Place, New York. 1852. Listed in the Table of Contents as: Chapter XIX. Charges for Dispatches from New York to all parts of the United States and Canada. Cost of Transmitting Telegraphic Messages. Page 187 onwards. Appears as Chapter XX: Charges for Telegraph Dispatches, Pages 189 to 194

References

Bagehot, W. "The Only Game in Town," *Financial Analyst's Journal*, 1971.

Blondheim, Menahem, "News over the Wires. The Telegraph and the Flow of Public Information in America, 1844–1897."

Blume, E. Marshall, Siegel, J. Jeremy and Rottenberg, Dan, "Revolution on Wall Street. The Rise and Decline of the New York Stock Exchange."

Bodenhorn, Howard "A History of Banking in Antebellum America: Financial Markets and Economic Development in an Era of Nation-Building (Studies in Macroeconomic History)." Cambridge University Press 2000.

Bodenhorn, Howard "State Banking in Early America: A New Economic History." Oxford University Press, USA 2002.

Branch, Ben and Freed, Walter, "Bid-Ask Spreads on the AMEX and the Big Board," *Journal of Finance*, Vol. 32, No. 1, 1977.

Cohen, Kalman J., Maier, Steven F., Schwartz, Robert A. and Whitcomb, David K., "The Microstructure of Securities Markets."

Copeland, E. Thomas and Galai, Dan, "Information Effects on the Bid-Ask Spread," *Journal of Finance*, Vo. 38, December 1983.

Davis, Lance, "International Capital Movements, Domestic Capital Markets, and American Economic Growth, 1865–1914, Chapter 3," *Working Paper.* July 19, 1996 Version.

Demsetz , Harold, "The Cost of Transacting," *Quarterly Journal of Economics* (1968).

DuBoff, R. B., "The Telegraph and the Structure of Markets in the United States, 1845–1890," *Research in Economic History*, Vol. 8, 1983, pp. 253–277.

S. Garg, *The Telegraph and Stock Exchanges*, Palgrave Studies in Economic History, https://doi.org/10.1007/978-3-031-40407-8

Garbade, Kenneth D. and Silber, William L., "Technology, Communication and the Performance of Financial Markets: 1840–1975," *The Journal of Finance*. Vol. XXXIII, No. 3, June 1978.

Garg, Sonali, "Innovations in Communications Technology and the Structure of Securities Markets: A Case Study of the Telegraph and the Rise of the NYSE to Preeminence. 1830–1860." *PhD Dissertation*, 2000. The Ohio State University.

"Inducements For Order Flow": *A Report To The Board of Governors, National Association Of Securities Dealers, Inc.* July 1991.

Jack, Treynor L., "Dealers in Securities," *The New Palgrave Dictionary of Money and Finance*. Edited by Peter Newman, Murray Millgate, and John Eatwell, 1992, Vol. 1.

Jegadeesh, Narasimhan and Subrahmanyam, Avanidhar, "Liquidity Effects of the Introduction of the S&P 500 Index Futures Contract on the Underlying Stocks," *Journal of Business*, Vol. 66, No. 2, 1993.

Jones, Alexander, "Historical Sketch of the Electric Telegraph: Including its Rise and Progress in the United States." George P. Putnam, 10 Park Place, New York. 1852.

Kindleberger, Charles P., "The Formation of Financial Centers: A Study in Comparative Economic History."

Kliedson, W. Allan and Werner, M. Ingrid "Round the Clock Trading: Evidence from U.K. Cross—Listed Securities," *Research Paper No. 1234R*. Institute for International Economic Studies and National Bureau of Economic Research.

Madhavan, Ananth, "Trading Mechanisms in Securities Markets," *Journal of Finance*, Vol. 47, No. 2, June 1992, pp. 607–641.

Mendelson, Morris and Peake, W. Junius, "Intermediaries or Investors': Whose Market Is It Anyway?" *Journal of Corporation Law*, 9 September 1994, pp. 443–481.

Nonnenmacher, Tomas W. "Law, Emerging Technology, and Market Structure: The Development of the Telegraph Industry, 1838–1868." *Ph.D. Dissertation*, 1995.

Peake, W. Junius, "Brother, Can you Spare Me a Dime? Let's Decimalize the U.S. Equity Markets," *Global Equity Markets: Technological, Competitive, and Regulatory Challenges*, Edited by Robert A. Schwartz, Chapter 19.

Peter, Rousseau L. and Richard, Sylla, "Emerging Financial Markets and Early US Growth," *Explorations in Economic History*, Vol. 42, 2005, pp. 1–26.

R.C. Michie, "The London and New York Stock Exchanges 1850-1914"

Roll, Richard, "A Simple Implicit Measure of the Effective Bid-Ask Spread in an Efficient Market," *The Journal of Finance*, Vol. 4, September 1984.

Shwartz, A. Robert, "Market Makers," *The New Palgrave Dictionary of Money and Finance*. Edited by Peter Newman, Murray Millgate, and John Eatwell, 1992, Vol. 2.

Subrahmanyam, Avanidhar, "A Theory of Trading in Stock Index Futures," *The Review of Financial Studies*, Vol. 4, 1991.

Sylla, Richard, Wilson, Jack W. and Wright, Robert E., "Integration of Trans-Atlantic Capital Markets, 1790–1845." Springer 2006.

United States Department of the Interior. National Park Services. National Register of Historical Places Inventory—Nomination Form. New York Stock Exchange.

William, Brown O., Jr., Harold, Mulherin J. and Marc, Weidenmier D., "Competing with the New York Stock Exchange," *The Quarterly Journal of Economics*, Vol. 123, No. 4, November 2008, pp. 1679–1719.

Wright, Robert E., "The First Wall Street: Chestnut Street, Philadelphia, and the Birth of American Finance." University of Chicago Press 2005.

Wright, Robert E., "The Wealth of Nations Rediscovered: Integration and Expansion in American Financial Markets, 1780–1850." Cambridge University Press. 1st edition, 1 October 2009.

Index

S. Garg, *The Telegraph and Stock Exchanges*, Palgrave Studies in Economic History, https://doi.org/10.1007/978-3-031-40407-8

GPSR Compliance
The European Union's (EU) General Product Safety Regulation (GPSR) is a set of rules that requires consumer products to be safe and our obligations to ensure this.

If you have any concerns about our products, you can contact us on

ProductSafety@springernature.com

In case Publisher is established outside the EU, the EU authorized representative is:

Springer Nature Customer Service Center GmbH
Europaplatz 3
69115 Heidelberg, Germany

www.ingramcontent.com/pod-product-compliance
Ingram Content Group UK Ltd.
Pitfield, Milton Keynes, MK11 3LW, UK
UKHW022222051026
15624UKWH00002B/305
* 9 7 8 3 0 3 1 4 0 4 0 6 1 *